ESSAYS ON ANTISEMITISM, ANTI-ZIONISM, AND THE LEFT

D1598076

STUDIES IN ANTISEMITISM

Alvin H. Rosenfeld, *editor*

ESSAYS ON ANTISEMITISM, ANTI-ZIONISM, AND THE LEFT

JEAN AMÉRY

Edited by Marlene Gallner
Translated by Lars Fischer
Foreword by Alvin H. Rosenfeld
With an essay by
Irene Heidelberger-Leonard

Indiana University Press

This book is a publication of

Indiana University Press
Office of Scholarly Publishing
Herman B Wells Library 350
1320 East 10th Street
Bloomington, Indiana 47405 USA

iupress.org

© 2021 Klett-Cotta -J.G. Cotta'sche Buchhandlung Nachfolger GmbH, Stuttgart
Cover Photo: © Pavel Sticha

Manufactured in the United States of America

Cataloging information is available from the Library of Congress.

ISBN 978-0-253-05875-1 (hardback)
ISBN 978-0-253-05876-8 (paperback)
ISBN 978-0-253-05877-5 (ebook)

First printing 2021

Funded by:

 Zukunftsfonds der Republik Österreich | Future Fund of the Republic of Austria

 Österreichische Hochschülerschaft an der Universität Wien | Austrian Students Union at the University of Vienna

 Fakultätsvertretungen Sozialwissenschaften und Philosophie an der Universität Wien | Student Representatives Faculty of Social Sciences and Philosophy at the University of Vienna

 Institutsgruppe Germanistik an der Universität Wien | Student Representatives German Studies at the University of Vienna

 Institutsgruppe Geschichte an der Universität Wien | Student Representatives History at the University of Vienna

 Institutsgruppe Politikwissenschaft an der Universität Wien | Student Representatives Political Science at the University of Vienna

Studienvertretung Anglistik und Amerikanistik an der Universität Wien | Student Representatives English and American Studies at the University of Vienna

Contents

Foreword

Alvin H. Rosenfeld

Some writers speak compellingly about the truth of their time but then fade as times change. Others provide valuable insights into contemporaneous events but also have the gift of foreseeing and describing what may lie ahead. The truths they help us understand, in other words, are not confined in time and space but have a resonance that echoes well into the future. We read them and learn to our benefit what they have been through but also what might be in store for us.

It is uplifting when what we encounter in reading such authors brightens our lives. And it can be disheartening when the events and ideas they map on the page take us into territory that is forbidding. To read Jean Améry is to enter this dark territory. It can be daunting and distressing to go where he has been. And yet to forgo knowing what this author knew about human experience at its worst would be unwise, particularly so if the malign forces that brought about his suffering and that of countless others are not over and done with. As the chapters of this book reveal on virtually every page, the threats to human decency, dignity, and life itself that Améry contended with throughout his mature years have hardly faded. In the form of a revived and increasingly menacing antisemitism, they are a prominent and troubling feature of today's social and political reality.

Jean Améry is known to English readers today largely owing to a single book, *At the Mind's Limits: Contemplations by a Survivor on Auschwitz and Its Realities* (1980). With the appearance of this work, first published in German in 1966 as *Jenseits von Schuld und Sühne* (Beyond guilt and atonement), Améry established himself as one of the indispensable thinkers on the nature of Jewish fate and the complexities of Jewish identity during the Holocaust and beyond. A slim volume of only five essays, *At the Mind's Limits* offers strikingly original insights into life and death in the Nazi camps and profound reflections on the anguished and enduring legacy of that terrifying time. Drawing on his own experiences as an inmate of a Belgian prison as well as his incarceration in three different camps, Améry's autobiographical and philosophical writings on the ordeals he underwent are distinguished by a rare degree of intellectual vigor and moral courage. At their best, they rise to the level of the most penetrating work on the Holocaust by such other major essayists as Imre Kertész, Primo Levi, and Elie Wiesel.

To be a Jew, Améry wrote, was to be a dead man on leave, someone marked out to be murdered. That realization came to him as early as 1935, when, as a college student in Vienna, he first read the Nazi racial laws. The child of a Jewish father whom he never knew (he was killed as a soldier in World War I) and a Catholic mother, Améry, whose given name was Hans Maier, grew up in Austria with no connection to Judaism or any knowledge of himself as a Jew. All that changed with the advent of Nazi rule in Germany and the singling out of Jews as a pariah people. Whether he personally regarded himself as a Jew or not, the new racial laws defined him as one. In doing so, he realized, they put him under a death sentence. With a clear-eyed view of what was in store for him, he abandoned his native Austria for Belgium, where for a short time he carried out some minor tasks for the anti-Nazi resistance. When he was seized for these activities, it was soon discovered that he was guilty of a far more serious offense—that of being a Jew. As such, he was sent to prisons and camps in France and Belgium before being transported to Auschwitz, Dora, and Bergen-Belsen. The extremity of his experiences in these places marked him for the rest of his life and, over time, determined the course he would take as a writer: that of a "vehemently protesting Jew," or, as he sometimes described himself, a "catastrophe Jew."

Améry's mature writing career was brief—a mere twelve years—and, often in the form of rapidly written journalistic articles, focused much of his attention on prominent figures and events in contemporary European politics and culture. His most lasting work, though, returned him to his wartime experiences and took the form of essayistic reflections on the torments he underwent as a Jew under Nazi rule. He had managed to survive the worst of what he had been subjected to, yet he was never able to look on his victimization as a thing of the past. He who was tortured remained tortured, he insisted. The Nazi crimes and the trauma that accompanied them were irrevocable.

The trauma intensified in his later years as he observed something he never expected to witness: the return of openly voiced antisemitic passions in German social and political life. Under the guise of anti-Zionism, "the old, wretched antisemitism ventures forth," as he ruefully noted in the preface to the second edition of *At the Mind's Limits*. At anti-Israel rallies in German cities in the 1970s, Améry heard not only fierce denunciations of Zionism as "a global plague" but also repeated cries of "Death to the Jewish people." The fact that these primitive hatreds were voiced by young men and women of the left, his own political home, infuriated Améry. He had not expected to witness such a scandalous spectacle in postwar Germany, especially coming from people he had regarded as his friends and natural allies, but "the tide has turned. Again, an old-new antisemitism impudently raises its disgusting head, without raising indignation." Not one to remain passive in the face of such hostility, Améry stepped forth to voice his own indignation. "The political as well as Jewish Nazi victim, which I was and am, cannot be silent," he declared. And in essay after essay, he forcefully wrote in opposition to the old evil enacted by Hitler's Germany and in protest against its rehabilitation in the form of a strident and threatening anti-Zionism.

Knowledge of Zionism was no more a part of Améry's formative years in Austria than was knowledge of Judaism, and yet in his later years he became a passionate defender of Israel, especially against the country's adversaries on the left. In this respect, he stood out among German-language authors of his time, for his voice as a public supporter of the Jewish state's right to exist found few others to match it. In fact, he was the first to publicly denounce anti-Zionism as a new form of antisemitism in Germany.

The grounds for this stance were not fundamentally political or ideological in nature but existential. To a large extent, they were based in an awareness that antisemitism was an inherent part of European culture and persisted in the minds of many even after the end of Nazi rule. As he saw it, "the possibility cannot be ruled out that the systematic annihilation of large numbers of Jews could recur." Israel, he believed, was as sure a defense against such a fearsome recurrence as any of the Jews could hope to have. And yet, since its birth, Israel was the target of militant opposition by Arab countries in the Middle East and, to his horror, by many in Europe whose anti-Zionism was trumpeted as a necessary and even "virtuous" political stance.

Améry's commitment to Zionism, therefore, was in many ways a reaction to the anti-Zionism of his own day, which, he was convinced, was only the latest manifestation of an age-old and probably ineradicable hostility to Jews. He was deeply wary of it, particularly as he feared it was becoming socially acceptable again. "Hatred of Israel, if left to run its course . . . , can only serve the evil and unjust scourge of antisemitism," he wrote. He was dismayed by that prospect, and he fought against it vigorously, often by invoking the hatreds that had been directed against him as a Jew and whose scars he bore literally on his own flesh. And so he denounced it in the strongest of terms: "Anyone who questions Israel's right to exist is either too stupid to understand that he is contributing to or is intentionally promoting an über-Auschwitz."

The origins of Améry's anti-anti-Zionism are easy to decipher. He had almost no firsthand knowledge of Israel, did not speak or understand its language, was unacquainted with its culture, and had no particular connection to its dominant religion. A proud humanist and liberal thinker, he had no interest in Judaism and had little sympathy for what he called its "superstitions." He visited Israel only once, and that was for just a brief stay late in his life. What made him the uncompromising Israel advocate that he became was not cultural affinities or nationalist sentiment but the Auschwitz numbers tattooed on his left forearm. The message this brand conveyed to him was potent and mattered far more than whatever wisdom he might find in the Torah and Talmud. Simply stated, that deeply inscribed, never-to-be-eradicated message is that every Jew alive, whether he knew it or not, could be set upon, abandoned, cast out, murdered. He was fond of quoting Sartre—"What the anti-Semite wishes, what he prepares for, is the death of the Jew"—but Améry really needed no outside authority to support his conviction that all Jews everywhere were potentially imperiled. He was also convinced that whenever and wherever the lives of Jews were once again endangered, "there is a place on earth that would take them in, no matter what." That place was Israel. For this reason, Améry was entirely open about his devotion to the Jewish state: "The existence of no other state means more to me. . . . Israel must under all circumstances be preserved."

It shocked him, therefore, that Israel, a sanctuary for victims of past persecution and a necessary asylum for would-be victims, was constantly under attack, often by his own political compatriots. The terms they used to denounce the Jewish state—Israel was excoriated as a ruthless aggressor and oppressor, denounced as an overly militarized state guilty of acts of fascist violence, condemned as a brutish colonialist power, a bridgehead of American imperialism in the Middle East, an agent of capitalist conspiracies, and so on—all these denunciations were right out of the Marxist playbook. A long-standing member of the left himself, Améry was familiar with the ideological origin and formulaic nature of these terms and was convinced that their application to Israel was unfair and grossly off the mark. Moreover, he saw them as dangerous, for the steady defamation of Israel as a criminal state had the effect of demonizing the country and preparing the ground for its elimination. Nothing provoked Améry more than that nightmarish possibility. More than anything else in his last years, it spurred him on to raise his voice as a "vehemently protesting Jew" and brought about the writings that make up the chapters of this book.

Although produced almost half a century ago, these essays could not be more timely, for they speak to problems that not only troubled Améry in the 1960s and 1970s but have intensified in more recent years. Especially under the camouflage term of *anti-Zionism*, animosity to Jews and, especially, the Jewish state has escalated since the early 2000s and on a global basis. Such hatred has also become more lethal. Jews have been attacked and sometimes killed in Berlin, Burgas, Brussels, Caracas, Copenhagen, Malmo, Mumbai, Paris, Toulouse, and elsewhere. A number of these assaults, carried out by people acting on behalf of Palestinian or Islamist organizations, are examples of Middle Eastern terrorism exported to other parts of the world for ideological and political purposes. Other attacks have been the work of lone actors seemingly bent on doing harm to Jews for other reasons, some of them economic, some quasireligious, and still others simply inexplicable.

In recent years, and to the surprise of many, the United States has also witnessed the spread of aggressive antisemitic passions, as was graphically illustrated on August 12, 2017, at the infamous Unite the Right rally of white supremacists, neo-Nazis, and Klansmen in Charlottesville, Virginia. The slogans that accompanied this march—"End Jewish influence in America," "Jews will not replace us," "Jews are the children of Satan"—dismayed onlookers, who were unaccustomed to seeing such raw antisemitism displayed on the streets of American cities. Even worse, the mass shooting of people at prayer in a Pittsburgh synagogue, on October 27, 2018—the deadliest attack on Jews in American history—came as a great shock and drove home the realization that the United States, too, was not immune to acts of violent Jew-hatred. Its history has never been free of social biases against Jews and episodes of antisemitic violence, but compared to the situation of Jews in European and Middle Eastern countries, Jews in the United States have lived a relatively safe and normal life, especially in recent decades. Charlottesville and Pittsburgh, however, have set American Jewish nerves on edge, as have frequent reports of attacks on Orthodox Jews in sections of New York City, and a new sense of unease is now palpable in American Jewish communities.

The major perpetrators of the most destructive acts against Jews and Jewish institutions in Europe, South America, and the Middle East in recent years have been radicalized Muslims, although in some cases antisemitic acts have also been carried out by neo-Nazis, extreme populists and nationalists, and assorted street thugs. In the United States, the most potent antisemitic threat at the physical level right now is found chiefly among white nationalists, white supremacists, neo-Nazis, and others on the far right. While all these types existed in the Europe of Améry's day, they were, for the most part, less active in carrying out assaults against Jews than they have since become. Améry's deepest concern was not so much with them as with his fellow partisans on the left, whose ideological anti-Israel hostility, in combination with the irrational hatreds of Europe's traditional attitudes toward Jews, he saw as the most dangerous form of contemporary antisemitism. Their goals were clear to him. To the antisemites, the Jew must always be eliminated, he firmly believed. To the anti-Zionists, the Jewish state must be eliminated. And "leftists are now the most eloquent proponents of anti-Zionism in all its brutishness."

"How," he wondered, "did Marxist dialectical thought come to lend itself to the preparation of the coming genocide?" This last phrase stuns by the magnitude of the disaster that Améry saw in the offing. Was it an exaggeration to think about the future in these alarming terms? Not in Améry's view, for unless the fervor that fueled anti-Zionist antisemitism could be effectively checked among his former allies on the left, he was convinced they were bound on a destructive course. By focusing their militant and obsessive anti-Jewish "hallucinations" on the state of Israel, they were bent on singling out Jews once again for a calamity of historical proportions. He called it "Auschwitz on the Mediterranean." Determined to raise his voice against such a nightmarish prospect, Améry devoted some of the sharpest and most incisive of his analytical and polemical writings in his last years to opposing anti-Zionism, most especially as it sought to advance its goals in progressive circles under the banners of human rights, antiracism, and universal justice. A cosmopolitan thinker, Améry placed a high value on all these principles and defended them repeatedly in his writings, but not when they were being cynically exploited for political ends that he saw as noxious. In his own words: "Antisemitism in the guise of anti-Zionism has come to be seen as a virtue." Améry saw such a claim as bogus and malign, and he waged a determined battle against it in his late writings.

To anyone aware of the return of antisemitism in our own day, the pertinence of Améry's arguments will be obvious. A newly energized and increasingly pervasive hostility to Jews and the Jewish state has become a prominent and pernicious feature of contemporary social life and political opinion. It shows up in physical assaults on Jews and Jewish synagogues, schools, community centers, cemeteries, museums, and Holocaust memorials. These attacks, some of them resulting in fatalities, now number in the hundreds in countries across the globe. In addition, and in some of its most impassioned forms, as in certain churches, labor unions, NGOs, and popular media outlets, today's anti-Jewish animus focuses relentlessly on the state of Israel, sometimes going so far as to brand it a criminal entity akin to apartheid South Africa and Nazi Germany. Such anti-Israel passions find especially sharp political expression on numerous university campuses, where students are now regularly exposed to forms of hostility that range from the shouting down of Israeli speakers; to aggressive boycott, divest, and sanction (BDS) campaigns; to annual springtime hate-fests called Israel Apartheid Week. The ritualization of these anti-Israel activities has been going on for years on some campuses and has the effect of making anti-Zionism a "normal" part of the college experience for numbers of students. Faculty members in certain academic disciplines are also actively involved in the boycott movement, sometimes urging their universities to break collegial ties with Israeli universities and discouraging their students from doing study-abroad programs in Israel.

The aim of these anti-Israel activities at their most extreme is to demonize and delegitimize the Jewish state in ways that recall the marginalization and dehumanization of Jews in Nazi Germany. The propaganda effect of such defamation worked against the Jews during the Third Reich, and Améry believed that it could work once again, this time against the Jewish state and its supporters. And so he raised his voice tirelessly against both antisemitism and anti-Zionism and the growing links he observed between the two.

He was not alone in doing so. Closer to our own day, Per Ahlmark, a former deputy prime minister of Sweden, wrote that "anti-Semites of different centuries had always aimed at destroying the then center of Jewish existence. . . . Today, when the Jewish state has become a center of Jewish identity and a source of pride and protection for most Jews, Zionism is being slandered as a racist ideology." The aim of such slander is to reduce the state that Zionism founded to an entity unworthy of retaining a place within the family of civilized nations. More recently, other world leaders have also spoken out strongly against such bigotry, noting that anti-Zionism is nothing other than a reinvention of antisemitism. In October 2015, for instance, Pope Francis was emphatic in pronouncing against it: "To attack Jews is antisemitism, but an outright attack on the state of Israel is also antisemitism."

Améry wrote similarly about the threats that a revived antisemitism, often under the cover of anti-Zionism, would pose, and not only to Jews but also to postwar Western civilization at large. Reflecting on developments since his first book appeared, he noted, "When I set about writing, and finished, there was no antisemitism in Germany, or more correctly: where it did exist, it did not dare to show itself." As he looked about him, he recognized that those days were gone, and not only in Germany. Antisemitism was no longer hidden covertly in the shadows but was, once again, a threatening presence in the public sphere. If its most aggressive adherents were to gain still more prominence, the result, he was sure, would be a reinvigoration of eliminationist passions that could bring on new disasters. In his most severe vision of what such a turn might produce, he referred, chillingly, to "Auschwitz II."

It is a fearsome prospect and, one hopes, it will never come about. Meanwhile, Améry's writings, the product of its author's painfully intimate knowledge of Auschwitz, stand before us in all their argumentative urgency as admonition and warning. We would do well to take them seriously.

Alvin H. Rosenfeld

ESSAYS on ANTISEMITISM, ANTI-ZIONISM, and the LEFT

Introduction

Marlene Gallner

JEAN AMÉRY'S BOOKS are only the tip of a vast iceberg: his extensive oeuvre included, inter alia, some five thousand newspaper articles, which, if reprinted, would cover roughly fifteen thousand pages. Today, few are familiar with Améry's critique of antisemitism, anti-Zionism, and their pervasiveness among leftists. He tends to be known, if at all, for his reflections on what it meant to have been a victim of the Shoah. The latter were, to be sure, of crucial importance to him and doubtless bled into all his writings, but Améry pursued other interests too, and he emphatically rejected attempts to categorize him exclusively as a "professional Nazi victim." This collection of essays seeks to make a different dimension of Améry's oeuvre, his spirited interventions in West German public debate, accessible to an English-speaking audience. All Améry's essays dealing directly with antisemitism, anti-Zionism, and their pervasiveness among leftists, initially published between 1966 and 1978 in a variety of locations, are assembled in a single volume here for the first time.

The Historical and Biographical Context

Améry was born in Vienna on October 31, 1912, as Hans Maier. From an early age, he was raised just by his mother, Valerie Maier, née Goldschmidt, because his father, Paul Maier, had been killed in World War I while fighting in the Austro-Hungarian army. His father had been immensely proud of the fact that his Jewish ancestors had settled in Vorarlberg, Austria's westernmost region, many generations ago. Even so, Judaism never played any great role in Améry's upbringing. If anything, he was more familiar with Christian traditions; his mother was a Catholic. Améry officially resigned from the Jewish community in 1933, when he was twenty-one, a step he reversed in 1937, two years after the Nuremberg Laws came into force. Setting out as a writer and editor working for a literary magazine in Vienna (*Die Brücke*), he soon encountered discrimination and persecution.

The Nazi racial laws radically transformed his understanding of what it meant to be a Jew. Not unlike many highly acculturated German and Austrian Jews, Améry began to develop his self-understanding as a Jew as a result of his increasing rejection by, and eventual expulsion from, the German cultural sphere with which he had previously identified. As Sigmund Freud, the founding father of psychoanalysis and an outspoken critic of religion, who had to flee Vienna in 1938, told an interviewer, "My language is German. My culture, my attainments are German. I considered myself a German intellectually until I noticed the growth of anti-Semitic prejudice in Germany and in German Austria. Since that time I prefer to avow myself a Jew."[1] Améry argued that antisemitism prevented being a Jew from being a matter of volition and turned it into an externally imposed obligation. As he noted in his essay "On the Impossible Obligation to Be a Jew," "I have gradually come to understand that it does not ultimately matter whether one can define one's existence in positive terms. As Sartre already pointed out some time ago, one is a Jew if one is identified by others as a Jew."

In 1938, after the *Anschluss*, Austria's incorporation into the Greater German Reich, Améry fled to Belgium. Two years later, he was imprisoned in an internment camp in southern France but was able to escape and returned to Brussels, where he joined the Belgian resistance movement. In 1943, he was caught distributing leaflets with anti-Nazi propaganda, rearrested, and taken to the detention camp Fort Breendonk, where, as a political prisoner, he was brutally tortured. When his captors realized that he was Jewish, he was deported to Auschwitz Monowitz and, from there, as the Red Army advanced, to a number of other concentration camps before eventually being liberated in Bergen-Belsen. Whereas, as a political prisoner, he had still been an individual, as a Jewish prisoner he had become a mere cipher, and the treatment to which he was subjected no longer bore any relation to what he might or might not have done.

On April 29, 1945, Améry arrived in Brussels again. Well into the 1960s, Améry earned his keep with writing commissions, mostly for the Swiss news agency Dukas. He certainly had no intention of publishing anything in Germany or Austria, the countries of the perpetrators. Indeed, to illustrate his dissociation from German culture, he changed his name from Hans Maier, or Mayer, as he preferred to spell it, to the French anagram Améry.

In the early 1960s, the Eichmann trial in Jerusalem and the Auschwitz trials in Frankfurt drew considerable attention, suggesting that the West German public was finally beginning to confront the issue of the Shoah. Against the backdrop of this emerging change in attitudes, Améry was able to find his own voice and for the first time speak openly about his experiences as a Jewish victim of the Nazis, thanks in no small measure to the support of Helmut Heißenbüttel, who, at the time, worked for the Süddeutscher Rundfunk, a large West German public radio station. He gave Améry the opportunity to record his autobiographically grounded reflections for the broadcaster's listeners. Five essays aired between October 1964 and April 1966 and concluded with "On the Impossible Obligation to Be a

---

1 George Sylvester Viereck, "Cheerful Humility Mark of Freud at 70 Years. Father of Psycho-Analysis Looks Brightly upon World as He Works to Rebuild Fortune," *The Sun* (Baltimore), August 2, 1927, SF8.

Jew." They were subsequently made available in print as *Jenseits von Schuld und Sühne* (available in English as *At the Mind's Limits: Contemplations by a Survivor on Auschwitz and Its Realities*). The book, first published by Gerhard Szczesny in Munich, quickly earned Améry considerable acclaim and is, to this day, his best-known publication.

With the book's success came the opportunity to publish his perspicacious analyses of current affairs in various West German quality newspapers and journals. In this context, he repeatedly took issue with contemporary antisemitism and was one of the first to raise the alarm about its extraordinary virulence among radical leftists and, especially, in the New Left. Throughout his adult life, Améry had considered himself a leftist, but he was now confronted with the fact that his former (ostensible) comrades-in-arms were inciting antisemitism. As a result, having lost his cultural home, Austria, in the 1930s, Améry also lost his political home. His already impaired trust in the world was further diminished, rendering his critique all the more acute.

The German public had initially been quite well disposed toward the young Jewish state, but this began to change from the mid-1960s onward and particularly so on the political left. In May 1967, anticipating the imminent Arab-Israeli war precipitated by the ongoing military threat Israel faced from its Arab neighbors, Améry wrote the essay "Between Vietnam and Israel," which eventually came out during the Six-Day War. It reads like an open letter to a left that fails to understand the Jews' unique situation. Améry also took issue with the left's escalating obsession with "American imperialism," which surely had little bearing on this case: "What is the point, in this context, of condemning American imperialism? To be sure, it exists, or, to be more precise, America absolutely is pursuing a policy of belligerent violence in Vietnam, but this has nothing to do with the crisis in the Middle East, where it is, after all, not the Americans who are threatening to wipe out a small country." Following the Six-Day War, left-wing antisemitism was no longer the preserve of Soviet loyalists. Eight years earlier, in 1959, the Socialist German Student League (SDS) had thrown its weight behind a groundbreaking exhibition on Nazi lawyers and judges who had been able to continue their careers in the postwar West German judiciary. The West German students openly took issue with the previous generation's Nazi past, which had previously drawn little critical attention. Yet, while the massive controversy precipitated by the students' determination to denounce the guilt and responsibility of West German public servants illustrated how important their initiative was, they were totally oblivious to the centrality of antisemitism to National Socialism. This allowed them to turn on the Jews with great speed and ferocity following the Six-Day War, and large parts of the nonaligned, so-called New Left soon embraced antisemitic positions. Before long, as the student movement in West Germany reached its zenith, demonstrators began calling for the death of Zionists. In December 1969, leftist activists in Kiel protested against a lecture by the Hebrew University's vice president for research, Alexander Keynan (a microbiologist), by distributing flyers with the infamous line "Strike the Zionist dead—make the East red!!"[2]

This new antisemitism took the guise of supposedly innocuous anti-Zionism, which struck many as virtuous since it seemed to be a matter of partisanship for the supposedly weaker party. In his first essay on the subject, "Virtuous Anti-semitism," published in July 1969, Améry severely criticized this development, exploring the nexus between antisemitism and anti-Zionism and refuting the notion that they were separable phenomena. Later that year, in "The New Left's Approach to 'Zionism,'" he took issue with the failure of many leftists to grasp how dangerous antisemitism was. Their particular brand of antifascism was per-ilously "oblivious to a number of phenomena specific to German National Social-ism, which the concept of fascism fails to encapsulate." On the one hand, they ignored the plight of the Jews and the threat of antisemitism; on the other, they were themselves beholden to well-established traditional antisemitic tropes, which they now directed at Israel. In "Jews, Leftists, Leftist Jews: The Changing Contours of a Political Problem," written in 1973, Améry's point of departure was the histori-cal bond between Jews and the left, which had now been severed. He was still plead-ing with the left, however. At the time, the left had become increasingly enamored of the various emerging national independence movements in Third World coun-tries, paying no attention to their in many cases authoritarian character. Améry was highly critical of the leftists' willingness to support authoritarian regimes in countries such as Algeria or Libya while demonizing Israel's alliance with the United States.

In his essay of 1976, "The New Antisemitism," Améry pointed to a particu-larly challenging aspect of the new antisemitism: "The antisemitism we are con-fronted with today does not speak its name. On the contrary: if one tries to hold it to account, it disowns itself." At the time, sections of the West German far left had become involved in the terror campaigns conducted by Palestinian organi-zations. Améry pointed to recent anti-Zionist kidnappings, the most prominent of which was the joint hijacking, in 1976, by German members of the Revolution-ary Cells and Palestinian members of the Popular Front for the Liberation of Palestine, of an aircraft on the way from Tel Aviv to Paris. The plane with its 248 passengers was diverted to Entebbe in Uganda, where the kidnappers separated the hostages into two groups, Jews and non-Jews, releasing only the latter. When one of the victims, who was a survivor of the Shoah, showed hijacker Wilfried Böse the number tattooed on his arm, Böse famously protested, "I'm no Nazi! . . . I am an idealist."

In 1976, Améry, who frequently commented on cultural events and develop-ments in West Germany, writing numerous reviews, voiced his concerns when

---

2 Wolfang Kraushaar, *Die blinden Flecken der 68er Bewegung* (Stuttgart: Klett-Cotta, 2018), 183.

Rainer Werner Fassbinder's play, *Der Müll, die Stadt und der Tod* (*Garbage, the City and Death*), was published (Fassbinder had aborted the rehearsals for its scheduled premiere in Frankfurt the year before). The play was an adaptation of Gerhard Zwerenz's novel *Die Erde ist unbewohnbar wie der Mond* (*The Earth Is as Uninhabitable as the Moon*, 1973). One of the figures in the play is a Jewish venture capitalist playing the property market. Fassbinder's resorting to this established antisemitic trope led to a heated national and international controversy. "Silliness is by no means invariably harmless," Améry noted in "Shylock, Kitsch, and Its Hazards," because "trash that dare not speak its name becomes kitsch, in other words: art, which is none." Hence, one would best serve the play simply by ignoring it, "were it not for its outright antihero, *the rich Jew*." Améry did not assume that Fassbinder had intentionally set out to harass Jews. Yet the play's skewed anticapitalist message all too readily lent itself to the promotion of antisemitism and that, surely, was dangerous. Améry's remarks were referenced in a report published in *Time* magazine on May 3, 1976 ("A Furor Over 'The Rich Jew'").

Seven years after the publication of his essay "Virtuous Antisemitism," Améry delivered an address with the same title on the occasion of Jewish-Christian Brotherhood Week, an event promoting Jewish-Christian understanding in (formerly West) Germany that has been taking place annually since 1952. This address was by no means just a rehash of the earlier essay. In it, he took issue with recent developments, such as the massive bias of the UN General Assembly and UNESCO against Israel, and highlighted the history of antisemitism in Muslim countries, which had (and has) all too often been downplayed. Améry called on the left "to reinvent itself by revisiting the problem of Israel, i.e., the Jewish problem." He also commented on his first (and only) visit to Israel in March of that year, stressing that what he had seen there had only confirmed his previous position: "No, I take back nothing. Far from it."

Améry's essay "The Limits of Solidarity: On Diaspora Jewry's Relationship to Israel" was published in *Die Zeit* in 1977. While it bears testimony to his unceasing commitment to Israel and his unrelenting opposition to anti-Zionism, it also demonstrates that Améry was determined to criticize specific political developments in Israel when he felt it was necessary to do so. When, in the 1970s, it was rumored that Arab prisoners were being tortured in Israeli prisons, Améry unambiguously warned against deploying such methods. For Améry, it was never in doubt that Israel had to exist as a Jewish state to ensure Jews the world over could take refuge there, should antisemitism force them to do so. Yet he found both the allegations of torture and the increasing reliance on religious rhetoric displayed by Menachem Begin, the new prime minister whose election had marked the end of the decades-long ascendancy of the Israeli left, profoundly unsettling.

The last essay in this volume is Améry's "My Jewishness," which draws extensively on autobiographical observations. It too was originally written for the radio. In May 1978, it was broadcast by the Süddeutscher Rundfunk, the same station that had aired "On the Impossible Obligation to Be a Jew," the essay that had introduced him to the West German public twelve years earlier. "My Jewishness" is one of the final texts Améry completed prior to his death. He committed suicide only five months later.

Why Read Améry Today?

Améry's observations are shockingly topical today, and his assessment of leftist antisemitism might just as well have been written specifically in response to the current situation. His perceptiveness in this regard is deeply unsettling. In the United States, as elsewhere, antisemitism, especially in the aforementioned guise of supposedly innocuous anti-Zionism, is being normalized to an alarming degree. Améry refuted the claim popular among antisemites that they are hostile not to Jews, whom they supposedly mean no harm, but merely to Israel by demonstrating the extent to which anti-Zionist views coincide with traditional antisemitic tropes and put all Jews at risk.

All too often, opposition to antisemitism and the commitment that Auschwitz should never repeat itself now amount to little more than lip service. They are rarely based on any meaningful understanding of the specific dynamics of antisemitism, and the profoundly misguided and misleading assumption that antisemitism is simply one particular form of racism has become commonplace. It underpins the skewed perception, based on the categorization of Jews as "white," that Jews today are less likely to experience discrimination than other minority groups. All too many outspoken antiracists are oblivious at best to the threats Jews face. Yet, as Améry pointed out repeatedly, drawing on Sartre's relevant observations, it is the antisemite who defines who will be persecuted as a Jew. In this sense, how those against whom the antisemitism is directed behave or what they look like is entirely irrelevant. This holds true both of Jews in general and of Israel in particular. Regardless of what it does, the Jewish state is assured of the anti-Zionists' hatred. The critique directed specifically by leftist academics and activists in the United States and elsewhere against Israel's liberal policies concerning lesbians, gay men, and transgender people is an obvious case in point.

Anti-Zionism is now more widespread among leftist academics and activists than ever. This renders Améry's emphasis, first articulated half a century ago, on the wrongheadedness of the widespread identification of Israel as an "aggressor and oppressor" all the more relevant. In "The New Left's Approach to 'Zionism,'" he stated unambiguously that "the antisemitism aroused long ago, presumably by the fallacious notion of the deicide, is as virulent as ever. . . . In the anti-Zionism of the Young Left it finds not only a well-functioning outlet but (supposedly) also an alibi. After all, the Jews have always had to play the bogeyman, the global foe."

Like the threats faced by Jews, so too the specificity of the Shoah and the eliminatory antisemitism underpinning it is increasingly being disregarded, and many consider the Shoah simply one among a variety of crimes against humanity. Améry issued a stark warning against the forgetfulness and repression of the past that facilitates the sort of generalizing "human rights" discourse that is then frequently deployed to agitate against the Jewish state.

Améry was adamant that the past needed to be taken seriously. Given that the attempt, undertaken on no rational grounds whatsoever, to totally annihilate the Jews had been made once, it could be made again. It was crucial not to underestimate the dangers inherent in antisemitism. The utter irrationality of the Shoah had been demonstrated by the fact that it had not only not hinged on what the victims had or had not done but that, toward the end of the war, the Nazis had ultimately given up on rational decision-making processes altogether, indeed, even on their own self-preservation, in order to prioritize the complete annihilation of European Jewry. The Shoah, then, was an unprecedented crime that would have seemed inconceivable before it occurred and so far continues to stand out in its singularity.

Améry demonstrated on a very practical level what it means to seriously pay heed to the new categorical imperative, which the Shoah, according to Adorno, has thrust on mankind: "to arrange their thoughts and actions so that Auschwitz will not repeat itself, so that nothing similar will happen."[3] As long as there is antisemitism in the world, another attempt to annihilate the Jews could be made—regardless of how irrational and improbable the threat might initially seem. Hence, Israel's role as a (potential) shelter from antisemitism remains indispensable. For all those who believe that obsessive criticism of the Jewish state benefits the supposedly weak, Améry's incisive analyses will make for instructive reading.

---

3 Theodor W. Adorno, *Negative Dialectics*, trans. E. B. Ashton (London: Routledge and Kegan Paul, 1973), 365.

Essays

Jean Améry

1 On the Impossible Obligation to Be a Jew (1966)

W<small>HEN AN INTERLOCUTOR</small>, in a conversation on some random topic, tries to drag me into a plural by incorporating me and referring to "us Jews," I frequently experience a sense of unease, which, while not exactly excruciating, is certainly deep-seated. I have long tried to fathom this squeamishness and psychological discomfiture, which has not been an easy task. Could it be, was it conceivable that, just as had been the case decades earlier when, wearing long white socks and lederhosen, I anxiously eyed my image in the mirror to ascertain whether it showed a comely German youth, that I, the former Auschwitz prisoner who had been given ample opportunity to recognize what he is and what he must be, still did not want to be a Jew? Of course not. It has been a very long time since I engaged in the folly of dressing up in the attire of what was, after all, actually my ancestral heritage. I am pleased that I neither was a German youth nor am a German man. However well the mask may once have suited me, it now lies in the junk room. I experience a rising sense of unease as soon as a Jew includes me, quite legitimately and as a matter of course, in his community, not because I do not want to be a Jew but because I do not know how. And yet I have no other choice. Nor do I merely submit to this obligation; I expressly insist on it as a part of my personality. It is the obligation to be a Jew and the impossibility of fulfilling that obligation that causes my vague anguish. This obligation and impossibility, this affliction and incapacity, are the subject of the present discussion. It is my unsure hope that the individual case will be sufficiently paradigmatic to be of concern also to those who neither are, nor are compelled to be, Jews.

Let me begin with the impossibility. If being a Jew means sharing a religious commitment with other Jews, participating in Jewish cultural and family traditions, and conforming to the ideal of Jewish nationalism, mine is a hopeless case. I do not believe in the God of Israel. I know very little about Jewish culture. I see myself as a boy trudging through the snow at Christmas to attend midnight mass. I do not see myself in a synagogue. I hear my mother calling out to Jesus, Mary, and Joseph when some domestic mishap occurred. No Hebrew evocations of the Lord ring in my ears. The image of my father, whom I hardly knew because he stayed where the emperor had sent him and his fatherland thought he was best placed, shows not a bearded Jewish scholar but a Tyrolean rifleman in a First World War uniform. I was nineteen by the time I learned of the existence of the Yiddish language. Conversely, I knew very well that, as far as our neighbors were concerned, my religiously and ethnically diverse family was Jewish and that none of us would have contemplated trying to deny or camouflage what could not be concealed anyway. Just as one of my fellow pupils was the son of a publican who had gone bankrupt, I was a Jew. When he was on his own, the downfall of his family's business may well have been of precious little concern to him. When he mixed with us or others, however, like us, he retreated into grudging awkwardness.

So, if being a Jew means sharing a cultural heritage and religious affiliation, I have never been a Jew and never will be. One might object that one can gain access to a tradition and enter into an affiliation and that one might therefore become a Jew of one's own free volition. Who could prevent me from learning Hebrew, reading Jewish history and literature, and participating in the religious and national rituals of the Jews as a nonbeliever? Well equipped with all the requisite cultural knowledge from the prophets to Martin Buber, I could move to Israel and call myself Yochanan. I am at liberty to choose myself as a Jew, and this liberty is both a uniquely personal and universal human privilege. Or so I am told.

Do I really have this freedom? I believe not. Would Yochanan, proudly bearing his new, self-acquired identity and steeped, say, in the knowledge of Hasidism, be immune to thinking of a Christmas tree adorned with gilded nuts on December 24? Would the upright Israeli who now speaks fluent Hebrew be able to eradicate entirely the youngster in the long white socks who was willfully flaunting an autochthonous dialect? The switching of identities plays an enormously stimulating role in modern literature. For me, it presented a challenge, which one either could or could not live up to with one's entire being. There could be no falling back on a provisional solution. It seems to me that in my case, the attempt to meet this challenge was in every respect doomed to failure. To be sure, one can reconnect with a tradition one has left behind. Crucially, however, one cannot simply invent one for oneself. Since I never was a Jew, I am not a Jew. And since I am not a Jew, I cannot become one. The Yochanan who is beset and transported back home by recollections of Alpine valleys and Glöckler processions when he sees Mount Carmel would be even more inauthentic than the youngster in the long white socks.[1] The dialectic of self-actualization, of being who one is by becoming who one is meant to become and wants to become, is closed off to me because being something in particular, not in the sense of some metaphysical essence but simply in the form of stored-up early experiences, invariably takes priority. Everyone has to be who he was in the earliest stages of his life, no matter how submerged they may later be. Nobody can become what he looks for in his recollections in vain.

I am not permitted to be a Jew, then. Given that I have to be a Jew all the same and this obligation prevents me from being anything other than a Jew, will I not

---

1 The Glöckler processions are a traditional event that takes place in the Austrian Salzkammergut on the night before Epiphany.

be able to find myself at all? Do I have to make do, in other words, without a history and exist as a shadow of nonexistent abstract universality, seeking refuge in the hollow formula that I am a human being? Not so fast. We are not quite there just yet. Since the obligation exists and is, moreover, supremely imperious, there may still be a way of overcoming its impossibility. After all, one wants to lead one's life without dissembling, as I did when I was undocumented and involved in the resistance movement, and without vanishing into some abstraction. A human being? To be sure, who would not want to be a human being? Yet one is only a human being when one is a German, a Frenchman, a Christian, a member of some community, however defined. I have to be a Jew and will be one, whether with or without religion, with or without being part of a tradition, whether as Jean, Hans, or Yochanan. Why this is so is the subject of this discussion.

The story did not begin with the boy being told by his fellow pupils, "You are really Jews all the same." Nor with the punch-up on the platform in front of the university when a Nazi's fist knocked out one of my teeth, long before Hitler came to power. "Indeed, we are Jews, but what of it?" I said to my school friend. My tooth today, yours tomorrow, and go to hell, the lot of you, I thought after the punch-up and bore the gap in my teeth proudly like an intriguing injury acquired during a duel.

It only began in 1935, when, poring over the paper in a café in Vienna, I studied the Nuremberg Laws, which had just come into force in Germany. I only needed to skim through them to realize that they applied to me. Society, in the guise of the National Socialist German state, which the world unquestioningly recognized as the legitimate representative of the German people, formally and with all possible clarity, had just made a Jew of me. Or rather, they had lent my preexisting knowledge of my Jewishness, which had previously been of little consequence, a whole new dimension.

What was this new dimension? This was not instantly obvious. Having read the Nuremberg Laws, I was no more Jewish now than I had been half an hour earlier. My features had not become more Mediterranean or Semitic, my range of associations was not suddenly filled with Hebrew references, the Christmas tree had not been transformed in an instant into a menorah. The verdict society had handed down to me, if it had any tangible impact, could only mean that I was henceforth given over to death. Of course, sooner or later, this holds true for all of us. But death had been promised that the Jew whom society and the law had now turned me into would become available sooner, in the midst of his days, each of which had become a reprieve, which could be revoked at any moment. I do not think that it is inadmissible, in the context of this discussion, for me to project Auschwitz and the Final Solution back into the year 1935. In fact, I am certain that it was indeed in this year, when reading the Nuremberg Laws, that I first took note of this death threat or, to be more precise, of this death sentence. Not that this required any great historical sensitivity, of course. Had I not on a hundred occasions heard the call for a German awakening combined with the request,

addressed to fate, that the Jews might perish? "Perish Judah!" had a rather different ring to it than the almost joyful *"L'aristocrat, à la lanterne!"*[2] Regardless of
whether one knew that this slogan was historically connected to the innumerable
pogroms of the past or took this into consideration, this was no revolutionary
hubbub. It was the carefully considered demand of a people concentrated in one
slogan, in a battle cry. Roughly at the same time, I also saw the photo of a Winter
Relief event in a city on the Rhine.[3] In it, in the foreground, taking pride of place
in front of the Christmas tree, which had been lit up electrically, was a banner
that read, "Nobody should go hungry, nobody should go cold, but the Jews should
croak . . ." Only three years later, when Austria was incorporated into the Greater
German Reich, I heard Joseph Goebbels baying on the radio that one should not
make a big deal of the fact that a few Jews were currently committing suicide in
Vienna.

I now understood that being a Jew meant being a dead man on furlough,
somebody who was to be murdered, who by mere coincidence was not yet where
he ought, by rights, to be. In this respect, although the danger has taken on
various guises and fluctuating degrees of intensity in the meantime, I have not
changed my mind since. What is generally referred to as the methodical "debasement" of the Jews by the Nazis reverberated in this death threat I grasped fully
for the first time when reading the Nuremberg Laws. Put differently: the expro-
priation of dignity expressed the death threat. For years we could read about it
on a daily basis. We were idle, evil, ugly, capable merely of misdeeds, and smart
only when we were bamboozling others. We were incapable of forming a state,
but neither were we capable of assimilating to the host peoples. Our bodies were
hirsute, fat, and bowlegged. Their mere presence sullied public swimming pools,
even park benches. Our loathsome faces, debauched and tainted by jug ears and
hanging noses, revolted the non-Jewish human beings who until yesterday had
been our fellow citizens. We were no longer deserving of kindness and therefore
no longer deserved to live either. We had only one right and one duty: to remove
ourselves from the world.

Sartre already offered a number of insights into this process of debasing the
Jew, which I am convinced amounted to a death threat long before Auschwitz,
in his study *Anti-Semite and Jew*, published in 1946. They are still valid. There
was no such thing as a "Jewish problem," he explained, but merely the problem
of antisemitism. The antisemite had cajoled the Jew into a position in which he
accepted the antisemite's image of him as his own self-image. Both insights are,

---

2 "The aristocrat to the lamp post!" is a line from *Ça Ira*, a song of the French Revolution.
3 Améry is alluding to the propagandistically charged activities of the so-called *Winterhilfswerk*
  established in September 1933 by the Nazis. Its purpose was the alleviation of social hardship by
  committing (non-Jewish) Germans to acts of charity toward other (non-Jewish) Germans.

to my mind, incontrovertible. Yet in his short phenomenological outline, Sartre was unable to offer a comprehensive account of the crushing pressure exerted by antisemitism and its ability to cajole the Jews into acquiescence. In fact, I suspect that the great author never fully grasped its irresistible force. In his attempt to evade his lot as a Jew, the Jew whom Sartre, without implying any value judgment, called "inauthentic," in other words, the Jew who has succumbed to the myth of the "universal human being," submits to the authority of his oppressor. In his defense, he did spend the years of the Third Reich with his back against the wall, and that wall too was hostile. There was no way out. After all, it is not as though merely the card-carrying radical Nazis revoked his dignity of being liked and with it his right to live. Germany in its entirety, or rather, the whole world gave its nod to this endeavor, though occasionally with a gesture of perfunctory regret.

Let us recall that after the Second World War, when large numbers of refugees from various communist countries headed westward, the states of what is known as the free world outdid each other in their willingness to admit and support them, and this although very few of them faced any immediate threat to life and limb in their home countries. Yet nobody wanted to let us in, even at a point in time when anyone of sound judgment should long since have appreciated what awaited us in the German Reich. It was therefore little wonder that the Jews, whether they were authentic or not, secure in the illusion of a God and nationalist anticipation or assimilated, were unable to muster much resistance when the enemy burned the imagery of Streicher's *Stürmer* into their skin.[4] Note, however, that this susceptibility had little to do with the established self-hatred of the German Jews who, prior to the outbreak of National Socialism, had been willing and wildly determined to assimilate. The self-haters had assumed that they could not be what they so desperately wanted to be: Germans. Hence, they despised themselves. They were unwilling to take on their existence as non-Germans, but no one forced them to repudiate themselves as Jews. The fact that it was precisely the brightest and most sincere Jews, authentic and inauthentic alike, who between 1933 and 1945 temporarily capitulated to Streicher, reflected a different kind of renunciation. It was no longer a question of morality but rather one of social philosophy. Presumably, they could not but acknowledge that the world sees us in a particular way, considers us idle, hideous, useless, and evil. Given this universal consensus, what was the point of objecting, of insisting that we were not in fact like that? The Jews' submission to the imagery of the *Stürmer* was no more than the acknowledgment of a social reality. Confronted with this reality, recourse to a form of self-evaluation that was entirely at odds with it must occasionally have seemed preposterous or foolish.

---

4 *Der Stürmer* was a Nazi newspaper devoted exclusively to the propagation of violent antisemitism, published by Julius Streicher from 1923 to 1945. Streicher was executed in Nuremberg in October 1946.

One does, however, need to have been there if one wants to participate in this discussion. When I recall that social reality, the wall of rejection that rose up before us wherever we turned, I have to think of my sojourn in Auschwitz Monowitz. Both in the camp and among the so-called free laborers who worked with us, a strict ethnically defined hierarchy was in place, which the Nazis had imposed on all of us. A Reich's German stood in higher regard than an ethnic German who was not a citizen of the Reich. A Fleming counted for more than a Walloon. A Ukrainian from the General Government fared better than a Pole. A worker from Eastern Europe was worse off than an Italian. The camp inmates found themselves right at the bottom, on the first rung, and the lowest among them, in turn, were the Jews. Even the most depraved non-Jewish career criminal outranked us. The Poles, regardless of whether they were genuine freedom fighters imprisoned after the ill-fated Warsaw uprising or just petty pickpockets, were united in their contempt for us. The same held true of the Belarusian workers, many of whom were barely literate. Yet Frenchmen too treated us with contempt. I can still hear the discussion between two Frenchmen, one of them a non-Jewish "free" laborer, the other a Jewish camp inmate. "*Je suis Français*,"[5] the latter stated. "*Français, toi? Mais, tu es juif, mon ami*,"[6] his compatriot responded dispassionately and without any hostility. A combination of fear and indifference had allowed him to learn the lesson that the German masters of Europe taught. I repeat: the world was content with the position the Germans had assigned to us, both the small world inside and the big world outside the camp. Rarely did the latter heroically stand up to be counted when, in the dark of night, we were taken from our flats in Vienna or Berlin, in Amsterdam, Paris, or Brussels.

Juxtaposed to the process of our debasement, which began with the proclamation of the Nuremberg Laws and led directly to Treblinka, was on our part, in my case, a symmetrical process of regaining one's dignity, a process that, for me, is still ongoing. In what follows, I try to make sense of the stages of this process. I invite the reader to accompany me for a short but tricky and treacherous part of the way. After all, what can be said about the dignity I was first denied in 1935, of which I was officially deprived until 1945, which one may not be willing to confer on me even now, and which I therefore have to create myself? What, for that matter, is dignity?

We might begin with an inversion of the identity I suggested earlier between debasement and death threat. Should I be right in assuming that the denial of dignity was in fact nothing other than the potential denial of the right to be alive, dignity and the right to life would be identical. Should I also be right in stating that the acknowledgment or denial of dignity depend on societal assent and that they constitute judgments that cannot be appealed by taking recourse to one's

5 Translation: "I am French."
6 Translation: "French, you? But you are Jewish, my friend."

own self-understanding, thus rendering any attempt pointless to convince the community intent on denying our dignity of its error on the grounds that we actually have a strong sense of our own dignity—if all this were true, any and every effort to regain one's dignity would indeed have been, and still would be, senseless. Debasement—that is, living under the threat of death—would be an inescapable fate. Fortunately, this logic is not entirely correct. To be sure, only society can confer dignity, be it the dignity of some office, the dignity of a profession, or the dignity of the citizen more generally. The claim that "I am a human being and as such I am possessed of dignity whatever you may do or say!," as long as it is asserted only within the individual, is a hollow mind game or delusion. However, the debased human being whose life is threatened can convince society of his dignity by not only taking on his lot, on the one hand, but by also rebelling against it, on the other. It is at this juncture that the logic of the sentence passed on him ultimately does not hold.

One must begin by unreservedly acknowledging the verdict society has handed down as a given reality. When I read the text of the Nuremberg Laws in 1935 and recognized not only that they applied to me but also that they were the concentrated textual and legal expression of the verdict German society had long since articulated with its "Perish!," I could have opted for intellectual flight, given my defense mechanisms free rein, and thus lost my claim to rehabilitation. I might have said to myself, "Well now, this is the will of the National Socialist state, of the German *pays legal*;[7] it has nothing to do with the real Germany, the *pays reél*.[8] It would not dream of expelling me." Or I might have argued that it was, after all, only Germany, one particular country, that had succumbed to this bloodstained delusion and taken the absurd decision to designate me, quite literally, as subhuman, while the world out there, the world at large with its Englishmen, Frenchmen, Americans, and Russians, fortunately, was immune to the collective paranoia that had befallen Germany. Or, finally, even without relying on the illusions of a German *pays reél* and a world immune to the German mental disorder, I might have afforded myself the comfort of saying to myself, "Whatever others may say about me is not true. Only my own self-perception and self-understanding is truthful. I am who I am for and within myself and nothing else."

I would not want to pretend that I did not occasionally succumb to this sort of temptation. What I can say with certainty, however, is that I did eventually learn to resist it and that even back then, in 1935, I already felt a muffled obligation to convince the world, a world that by no means broke off all relations to the Third Reich in unanimous outrage, of my dignity. I grasped, however vaguely, that I had to acknowledge the verdict for what it was, to be sure, but that I could

---

7 Translation: the country in its legal guise (i.e., the state).
8 Translation: the country as it actually is.

also force the world to reverse it. I acknowledged the value judgment but at the same time decided to overcome it by rebelling.

Rebellion, to be sure, is a big word. It might suggest that I was, or am without justification trying to present myself as, a hero. A hero is the last thing I was. When the small gray Volkswagen cars displaying POL on their number plates crossed my path,[9] first in Vienna and then in Brussels, fear took away my breath. When a Kapo raised his arm to beat me,[10] I did not stand still like a rock; I ducked. Even so, I did embark on the process of regaining my dignity, otherwise I would not have stood the slightest chance of surviving the horror, not just in physical but in moral terms too. There is not a lot I can say in my defense, but what there is, I do want to mention. I took it on myself to be a Jew, although there would have been ways of making alternative arrangements. I agreed to join a resistance movement whose realpolitikal prospects were slim indeed. And in the end, I regained a skill that I and people like me tended to have forgotten about but that was much more important than the moral strength to resist: the skill of returning a punch.

From my time in Auschwitz, I recall the foreman Juszek, a Polish career criminal of terrifying forcefulness. On one particular occasion, he hit me in the face for some trivial reason. This was how he was used to treating all the Jews working under him. I instantly sensed with piercing intensity that this was the time for me to move forward with my protracted appeal against society's verdict. In an act of outright rebellion, I hit the foreman Juszek in the face and imprinted my dignity on his jaw with my fist. That I, being physically much weaker, ultimately lost the fight and was brutally beaten was of no further concern to me. Beaten up and in pain, I was pleased with myself. This was not a matter of courage or honor; what concerned me was exclusively the fact that I had understood so well that there were moments in life when who one was and what the future would hold were concentrated entirely in one's body. In my hunger, in the blow I had suffered and in the blow I had inflicted, I was my body and nothing other than my body. My body, cadaverous and caked with dirt, was my predicament. When it braced itself to deliver a blow, my body *was* my physical and metaphysical dignity. In a situation like this, physical violence is the only means of resetting a dislocated personality. Both for myself and for my opponent, I was I as a blow. When I asserted my dignity in this particular social context by placing a punch in a human face, I was anticipating what I later read, expressed in theoretical terms, in Frantz Fanon's analysis of the behavior of the colonial peoples in *Les damnés de la terre*.[11] Being a Jew meant acknowledging that to flee from the death sentence passed down by the world into some kind of interiority, rather than

---

9 "POL" indicated these were police cars.

10 A Kapo was a prisoner functionary in a concentration camp who supervised other inmates.

11 *The Wretched of the Earth* (1961).

accepting it as the world's verdict, on the one hand, while at the same time physically rebelling against it, on the other, would be an ignominy. I became a human being not by inwardly laying claim to my abstract humanity but by identifying myself in the given social reality as a rebellious Jew and making this status wholly my own.

As I say, this process has been, and is, ongoing. As things stand, it has neither been successful nor failed. Following the collapse of the National Socialist Reich, there was a short window of opportunity when I felt justified in assuming the situation had been radically transformed. For a short moment, I was under the illusion that my dignity had been fully restored by my own modest activities in the Résistance, by the heroic uprising of the Warsaw ghetto, and, above all, by the contempt the world displayed toward those who had stripped me of dignity. It seemed possible that the denial of our dignity we had experienced had been a historical error, an aberration, a collective universal sickness from which the world had spontaneously recovered the moment the German generals capitulated to Eisenhower in Reims. I was soon disabused of my illusions. While one was still identifying the mass graves in which the Jews had been buried, antisemitic rioting erupted in Poland and Ukraine. In France, the traditionally susceptible petit bourgeoisie had allowed itself to be infected by the occupation forces. When survivors and refugees returned and laid claim to their former homes, simple housewives would occasionally state, with a peculiar mixture of satisfaction and annoyance, "*Tiens, ils reviennent; on ne les a tout de même pas tous tué.*"[12] Even in countries such as Holland, where antisemitism had previously been virtually unknown, in marked contrast to most of the Jews, a "Jewish problem," bequeathed by the German propaganda, now supposedly existed. England closed off Mandate Palestine for the Jewish would-be immigrants who had escaped the camps and dungeons. I soon had to recognize just how little had changed. For all that the potential executioners were showing considerable restraint for the time being or even vociferously condemning what had occurred, I was still slated to be murdered in the foreseeable future.

I certainly grasped this reality. But should I have allowed it to compel me to grapple, as one likes to say, with antisemitism? Certainly not. In their capacity as historical, socially conditioned intellectual phenomena, antisemitism and the "Jewish Question" neither were nor are any of my business. They are the antisemites' preserve, their ignominy, their sickness. It is they who need to master these issues, not I. I would be playing into their grubby hands were I to examine the role religious, economic, and other factors play in the persecution of the Jews. Were I to embark on inquiries of this kind, I would merely be succumbing to the intellectual conceit of historical objectivity with its assumption that those who

---

12 Translation: "Well, they are coming back; one has not killed *all* of them after all."

were murdered are as guilty as those who murdered them, if not more so. Having been wounded, I am beholden to disinfect and bandage my wound, not to contemplate why the thug raised the bludgeon and, having identified the reason, to work my way toward exculpating him.

The antisemites were not my concern; I was merely obliged to master my existence, which was hard enough. Certain options, which were available to me during the war, no longer existed. I could hardly run around in the first postwar years wearing a yellow star, at least not without seeming silly or eccentric (even to myself). Given that he was no longer as readily identifiable, the opportunity to thump the enemy in the face also ceased to exist. I still felt the desire and compulsion to regain my dignity with the same urgency as I had done during the war and the years of National Socialist rule, yet doing so proved inordinately more difficult in this climate of illusive peace. More clearly than I had done in the days when physical rebellion had been at least an option, I was now forced to grasp that I was faced with an impossible obligation.

At this juncture, I should pause for a moment and explain how I distinguish myself from all those Jews who do not speak against the backdrop of my own experiences. In his book *La condition reflexive de l'homme juif*,[13] the French philosopher Robert Misrahi has stated, "Henceforth, the Nazi catastrophe is the absolute and radical point of reference for all forms of Jewish existence." I certainly would not want to cast doubt on this statement. I am convinced, however, that not every Jew is capable of consciously confronting this nexus. Only those with experiences similar to mine can abide (by and with) the period between 1933 and 1945. I consider this anything but a matter of pride. It would be pretty laughable to claim credit for something that one did not do but merely endured. I assert and intimate my lamentable prerogative, if anything, with a sense of embarrassment. The catastrophe indeed forms an existential point of reference for all Jews, but only those of us who were sacrificed can intellectually retrace and draw out the catastrophic event. The others are free to empathize. They should indeed contemplate our fate, a fate that could have been theirs yesterday and may yet be theirs tomorrow. We will respect their intellectual efforts, though with a measure of skepticism, and in conversation with them, we will soon fall silent and think, Go for it, but try as you may, you will always sound like the blind man trying to describe color.

Which ends my digression and brings me back to being on my own in the company of just a few close comrades. It brings me back to the postwar years, which no longer gave us the opportunity to hit back (literally) because we were dealing with an adversity that no longer wanted to be all too explicit in speaking its name. And it brings me back to my impossible obligation.

---

13 Literal translation: the reflexive condition of the Jewish man.

It is obvious that its impossibility does not affect everyone. There are plenty of Jewish men and women, be they workers in Kiev, businessmen in Brooklyn, or farmers in the Negev, whose Jewishness always has been, and continues to be, a positive fact. They speak Yiddish or Hebrew. They keep the Sabbath. They elucidate the Talmud or stand to attention as young soldiers under the blue-and-white banner adorned with the Star of David. For them, being a Jew means being part of a community, be it in a religious or national sense or simply as a result of their individual reverence for the portrait of their sidelock-bearing grandfather. As an aside, one might perhaps ask, as the French sociologist Georges Friedman has done, whether the same will hold true of their descendants too or the demise of the Jewish people is perhaps on the horizon, both in the Mediterranean country, where the Israeli is superseding the Jew, and in the diaspora, where the Jew could be totally integrated, not so much into the host peoples who are themselves losing their national character but into the greater unity of the technical-industrial world.

I shall not endeavor to answer this question. I have no strong feelings about the persistence or disappearance of the Jewish people as an ethnic-religious community. There is no room in my discussion for those Jews who are Jews because their tradition offers them a sense of security. I can speak only for myself—and, not least, though cautiously, for the likely millions of contemporaries on whom their Jewishness was thrust by force majeure and who have to contend with it with no God, no history, and no Messianic-nationalist anticipation to assist them. For them, for me, being Jewish equates to feeling the burden of yesterday's tragedy within oneself. I bear the number from Auschwitz on my left forearm. While shorter, it is nevertheless more exhaustive in its disclosure and offers a more authoritative fundamental characterization of Jewish existence than the Pentateuch or the Talmud. When I tell myself, the world in general, and the religious and nationalist Jews who do not acknowledge me as one of their number in particular that I am a Jew, I am referring to the realities and options distilled in that number from Auschwitz.

In the course of the two decades that have passed since my liberation, I have gradually come to understand that it does not ultimately matter whether one can define one's existence in positive terms. As Sartre already pointed out some time ago, one is a Jew if one is identified by others as a Jew. Max Frisch has since offered a stark dramatization of this insight in *Andorra*.[14] This insight is still valid, but it is perhaps worth adding the following clarification. Even when I, unlike the poor wretch in *Andorra*, who would like to be a carpenter but is only given the option of being a merchant, am not identified by others as a Jew, I nevertheless

---

14 *Andorra* (1961) is a play by the Swiss playwright and novelist Max Frisch. The principal protagonist, Andri, despite not actually being Jewish, is assumed to be, and is eventually murdered as, a Jew.

am a Jew simply because my environment does not expressly identify me as a non-Jew. Being something can mean *not* being something else. The fact that I am not a non-Jew makes me a Jew; it both compels me to be a Jew and obliges me to embrace the fact that it is so. I am obliged to accept that I am a Jew and to affirm this fact in my everyday existence, be it by intervening and nailing my colors to the mast when people make stupid remarks about Jews at the greengrocer's, by addressing unknown listeners on the radio, or by writing magazine articles.

Yet, for me, being a Jew does not exhaust itself in bearing within me the catastrophe that has occurred and may conceivably recur. Above and beyond this commission, it also equates to *fear*. Each morning affords me the opportunity to scan the number from Auschwitz on my forearm as I get up. This strikes at the deepest recesses of my being; indeed, I am not entirely sure that it is not in fact my entire being. It affects me almost as intensely as being hit by a policeman's fist for the first time once did. Every day anew, I lose my trust in the world. The Jew whose Jewishness is not positively defined—we may confidently call him the catastrophe Jew—is forced to get by without trust in the world. My neighbor greets me with a friendly, "*Bonjour, monsieur.*"[15] "*Bonjour, madame,*"[16] I reply and doff my hat. Because another *madame* looked away yesterday when a *monsieur* was taken away, and another *monsieur*, like a stone angel from some bright and severe heaven to which the Jews will never have access, watched a *madame* through the bars of a departing vehicle, worlds now separate *monsieur* and *madame*. I read an official notice that calls on "*la population*" to act in a particular way: to put out their bins on time, say, or to fly a flag on a particular national holiday. Great fear prevented *la population* from hiding me yesterday, and whether it would show more courage if I came knocking tomorrow is, alas, a moot point. Hence, *la population* too constitutes yet another extraterrestrial realm I can no more hope to enter than I might Kafka's castle.[17]

Twenty years have passed since the catastrophe. They have been years of great honor for our sort, characterized by an abundance of Nobel laureates, French prime ministers called René Mayer or Pierre Mendès-France, and an American UN ambassador called Goldberg, who pushed anti-Communist American patriotism of the most wholesome kind. The human rights declarations, the democratic constitutions, the free world and free press—all this seems too good to last. Nothing can lull me into the sense of security again of which I was disabused in 1935.

As a Jew I go through life like a sick man afflicted by one of those illnesses that cause few symptoms but are invariably terminal. Not that he has always had

---

15 Translation: "Good day to you, sir."
16 Translation: "Good day to you, madam."
17 This is a reference to Franz Kafka's novel *The Castle* (1926). Its protagonist faces immense difficulties trying to enter the castle and talk to the clerks residing there.

this illness. When he tries to find his ego by peeling away the layers, as though, like Peer Gynt,[18] peeling an onion, he cannot find the cause of the problem. Neither his first school day, his first love, nor his first poems had anything to do with it. Yet now he is a sick man, more so and more intensely so than he may be a tailor, a bookkeeper, or a poet. I too am precisely what I am not because, before I became one, I was not, before all else, a Jew. The death, which the sick man will not be able to elude, is the menace looming over me. They greet each other, saying, "*Bonjour, madame,*" "*Bonjour, monsieur.*" Yet since the woman cannot take over her sick neighbor's infirmity and die of it herself, they remain strangers.

Lacking trust in the world, as a Jew I am alienated and isolated from my environment. All I can do is come to some sort of arrangement with this alienation. I must accept it as an essential element of my personality and insist on it as though it were an inalienable possession. Even now, I am engulfed by loneliness every day. I have been unable to trouble yesterday's murderers and tomorrow's potential aggressors with the moral truth of their misdeeds because the world as a whole did not assist me in doing so. Hence, I am as alone as I was when I was being tortured. Those who surround me now I do not, however, consider my adversaries, as I did my torturers. They are not against me; they simply exist alongside me, unaffected by me and the menace that slinks around with me. As I walk past I greet, and feel no hostility toward, them. They offer me no security. Only the fact that I am, in a manner that defies positive definition, a Jew does so. It is my burden and my prop.

The commonality, such as it is, that exists between me and the world whose as yet unrevoked death sentence I acknowledge as a social reality is polemical in nature. You do not want to listen? So listen. You are not interested in the havoc your indifference has the potential to wreak at any point both on you yourself and on me? What occurred is of no concern to you because you did not know about it or you were too young or had not even been born? You should have seen. Your youth affords you no carte blanche, and you need to break with your father.

Once again, I am compelled to ask myself the question I already touched on briefly in my analysis of ressentiment.[19] Could it be that I am mentally ill, that I am afflicted by an incurable sickness, by mere hysteria? The question is purely rhetorical. I have long since answered this question conclusively. I know

---

18 Peer Gynt is the protagonist of Henrik Ibsen's eponymous play (1867). The peeling of the onion takes place at the beginning of act 5, scene 5.

19 In the previous chapter of *At the Mind's Limits*, "Ressentiment," which he had previously recorded for the public broadcaster Süddeutscher Rundfunk, where it was transmitted on March 7, 1966, Améry developed an idiosyncratic concept of resentment as the obligation he felt as a survivor not to grant the perpetrators of the Shoah forgiveness. The German word for resentment, *Ressentiment*, is instantly recognizable as a foreign loan word and indicates a sophisticated linguistic register—and therefore stands out in way that the English word *resentment* does not. Hence the decision to translate it as *ressentiment* to emphasize its contextual specificity.

that I am afflicted not by a neurosis but by actual circumstances of which I have a precise understanding. I was not having hysterical hallucinations when I heard the shouts of "Perish!" or, as I passed by, witnessed people opining that the Jews must surely have been up to something, otherwise one would hardly treat them so harshly. "They are being arrested, so they must have done something wrong," I heard a respectable Social Democratic working-class woman say in Vienna. "What one is doing to the Jews is so cruel, *mais enfin* . . . ,"[20] I heard a sympathetic patriot speculate in Brussels. I can only conclude that it is not I who was, or is, disturbed. It is in fact the historical development that is neurotic. It is the others who are mad, and I stand among them, perplexed, like somebody who is entirely sane and, having joined a guided tour through a psychiatric clinic, has suddenly become separated from the psychiatrists and minders. And yet, the verdict handed down by the insane could be executed at any time; I have absolutely no recourse against it, and my own clarity of mind is entirely irrelevant.

My discussion is drawing to a close. I have explained how I position myself in the world; I now need to say something about the ways in which I relate to my brethren, the Jews. One might ask whether they really are my brethren. To be sure, the fact that my external appearance to some extent displays what a race scientist might identify as Jewish features could be relevant if I were caught up in a crowd hounding Jews hep-hep style. When I am left to my own devices, however, or find myself in the company of other Jews, it becomes a nullity. Do I have a Jewish nose? If so, it might indeed get me into trouble in a hep-hep-style situation. And yet it would in no way connect me to even one other Jewish nose on the planet. Whether I indeed look Jewish, and I am not sure one way or the other, is of interest only to others. Only the way in which they objectively position themselves toward me makes this an issue that affects me too. Even if I looked as though I had stepped straight out of Johann von Leers's book *Juden sehen Dich an*,[21] this would not render the suggested commonalities between me and other Jews real in any way I could subjectively validate. It might create a community of fate between me and other Jewish human beings, but it would establish no positive commonality between us. All I am left with is the intellectual or, to be more precise, the consciously perceived nexus between Jews, Jewishness, and me.

---

20 *Mais enfin* translates as "but in the end."

21 Johann Leers joined the Nazi party in 1929 (and later the SS). He was appointed to the University of Jena as a professor of racial history in 1939. He played a key role in the production and circulation of antisemitic propaganda. *Juden sehen Dich an* (lit. Jews are looking at you), which supposedly illustrated the depravity of "the Jew" with portraits of various Jews and Jewish personalities, was published in 1933. It was dedicated to Julius Streicher. After the war, Leers continued to spread antisemitism with all means at his disposal, first in and from Argentina, then in and from Egypt, where he converted to Islam.

As I already stated preemptively at the outset, this nexus is a nonentity. I share virtually nothing with other Jews *qua* Jews: no linguistic or cultural tradition, no childhood memories. In the Austrian Vorarlberg, there had lived a landlord and butcher who, so I was told, had spoken fluent Hebrew. He was my great-grandfather. I never met him, and he must have died the best part of a century ago. Prior to the catastrophe, my interest in Jews and matters Jewish was so minimal that I would be hard-pressed to say which of my acquaintances at the time were or were not Jews. Whatever I undertook to try and make Jewish history or culture my own or to identify personal reminiscences in Jewish folklore was invariably doomed. The environment I had inhabited in the years in which one learns to be oneself was simply not Jewish, and there is no way of undoing this. Yet the futility of my search for a Jewish self in no way undermines my sense of solidarity with every single endangered Jew the world over.

I read in the papers that an illegal bakery for unleavened Jewish Passover bread has been discovered in Moscow, and the bakers have been arrested. Now, I am slightly less interested in the Jews' ritual *matsot* as a foodstuff than I am in crispbread. I nevertheless find the actions of the Soviet authorities unsettling and outrageous. Some American country club, I am told, will not admit Jews as members. While I would not under any circumstances want to join this patently dreary bourgeois association, the cause of the Jews demanding admission is definitely mine. I have never visited the state of Israel and do not have the slightest intention of living there, but the demand of some Arab statesman that Israel be wiped off the map cuts me to the quick. My solidarity with all Jews whose freedom or equality, not to mention their physical existence, are under threat is *also* but by no means *only* a response to antisemitism, which, as Sartre has pointed out, is not some opinion but the predisposition and willingness to engage in the crime of genocide. This solidarity forms a part of my personality and a weapon in the struggle to regain my dignity. Only once, despite not being a Jew in some positively defined sense, I become a Jew in full knowledge and acknowledgment of the world's verdict against the Jews and eventually participate in the historical appeals process against this verdict, am I permitted to use the term *freedom*.

This solidarity in the face of adversity is all that connects me with my Jewish contemporaries, be they believers or nonbelievers, nationalists, or assimilationists. They consider this little or nothing. For me and my continued existence, it means a great deal, most likely more than my grasp of Proust's books, my affection for Schnitzler's novellas, or my enjoyment of the Flemish landscape. Without Proust and Schnitzler and the poplars bending in the wind by the North Sea, I would be poorer than I currently am, but I would still be a human being. Without my sense of belonging to the endangered Jews, I would be a refugee giving up on himself in the face of reality.

I say reality because this, for me, is the decisive point. Whether the antisemitism, which has turned me into a Jew, is or is not a form of madness is not my concern in this instance; it is, however, regardless, a historical and social fact. I was actually in Auschwitz and not just in Himmler's imagination. And antisemitism still exists. One would need to be utterly blind to our social and historical circumstances to deny this. This holds true of its heartlands, Austria and Germany, where the Nazi war criminals are either not prosecuted at all or receive laughably short prison sentences, of which they serve barely a third anyway. It exists in England and in the United States, where one tolerates the Jews but would be not at all displeased to be rid of them. It exists, in the guise of nationalist anti-Zionism, in the Arab states. It exists, with considerable consequences, in the intellectual universe of the Catholic church. The complexity and confusion that characterized the deliberations of the Council on the so-called Jewish declaration was painfully embarrassing, the valiant efforts of quite a few church dignitaries notwithstanding.

It is conceivable, of course, although the current circumstances make it far from likely, that the final act of the historical drama that is the persecution of the Jews was played out in the Nazis' death camps. It seems to me, however, that the dramaturgy of antisemitism persists. The possibility cannot be ruled out that the systematic annihilation of large numbers of Jews could recur. What, I wonder, would happen if the Arab countries, which have been armed by East and West alike, were to clinch a total military victory over the tiny state of Israel? What sort of place would America be not just for the negroes but also for the Jews if it succumbed to military fascism? What would have happened to the Jews in the European country that currently has the largest Jewish population, in France, if, in the early years of this decade, not de Gaulle but the OAS had been victorious?

It is with considerable unease that I read the following definition of what characterizes a Jew in the study of a very young Dutch Jew: "A Jew can be described as somebody who is more anxious, distrustful and irritable than his fellow citizen who has never been persecuted." This seemingly valid definition is rendered erroneous by the fact that its author has left out an indispensable addendum, which should read, ". . . because he has good reason to assume that a new catastrophe could occur any time." The awareness of yesterday's cataclysm and the legitimate anticipation of its possible future recurrence constitute the ultimate vanishing point. Bearing both of them within me, and the latter twice over because I barely escaped the former, I am not "traumatized," I am facing up to reality in an intellectually and psychologically entirely appropriate manner. My awareness of the fact that I am a catastrophe Jew is not an ideological construct. It is similar to the class consciousness Marx sought to reveal to the proletarians of the nineteenth century. Being who I have become, I am subject to, and illustrate, a historical reality of my age; and given that I was subjected to it more profoundly than most of my brethren, I am also in a better position to throw a light on that reality. I can neither take credit for this nor is it a matter of intelligence; it is a lot assigned by happenstance.

All this would be easier to bear if more connected me to other Jews than my rebellious solidarity, if the obligation would not constantly come up against the impossibility of its realization. I am only too aware of this problem. I once sat next to a friend during a performance of Arnold Schoenberg's "A Survivor from Warsaw."[22] When the choir, in unison with the trombone, began to sing the "Sh'ma Yisrael,"[23] my companion turned white as a sheet, and beads of sweat began to form on his forehead. My heart beat no faster than usual, but I felt needier than the comrade on whom the Jewish prayer sung among the blasts of the trombone had made such a profound impression. For me, I thought later, being a Jew cannot be about some form of emotionally charged reverence but only about fear and, when fear, in order to acquire dignity, turns into ire, about ire. "Hear, O Israel" has nothing to do with me. All that wants to burst out of me is an enraged "Hear, O world." This is what the six-digit number on my forearm and the sense of catastrophe that dominates my existence demand.

I have often interrogated myself as to whether it is possible to lead a truly human life under the pressure of being caught between fear and ire in this way. Those who have followed my line of thought may well assume that the author is an ogre, if not of vengefulness then of bitterness. There may be a kernel, though indeed no more than a kernel, of truth in this assumption. A man who endeavors to be a Jew in the manner in which I do so and under the circumstances imposed on me, who seeks to concentrate and frame the reality of the so-called Jewish Question within himself by elucidating his own existence as it is shaped by the catastrophe, is totally incapable of naïve trust. No human mead will run from his lips, and he will engage in gestures of generosity only with great difficulty. Yet none of this implies that his fear and ire force him to be less virtuous than his ethically inspired contemporaries. He can, and does, have friends; he is friendly not least with nationals from the very peoples who placed him in the sling in which he vacillates between fear and ire. He can also read books and listen to music like the unharmed, and he does so with equal sensitivity. In matters of morality, he is likely to be tetchier than his fellow men when it comes to all forms

---

22 Arnold Schoenberg wrote and composed *A Survivor from Warsaw for Narrator, Men's Chorus and Orchestra*, op. 46, in 1947 as "a warning to all Jews, never to forget what has been done to us—never to forget that even people who did not do it themselves, agreed with them and many of them found it necessary to treat us this way." Letter to Kurt List, November 1, 1948, http://archive.schoenberg.at/letters/search_show_letter.php?ID_Number=4802.

23 The "Sh'ma Yisrael" (based on the text of D'varim/Deuteronomy 6:4) stresses the oneness of God and is one of the most important (and best-known) Jewish prayers. As Schoenberg wrote in the letter mentioned in the previous footnote, "The Shema Jisroel at the end has a special meaning to me. I think, the Shema Jisroel is the 'Glaubensbekenntnis,' the confession of the Jew. It is our thinking of the one, eternal, God who is invisible, who forbids imitations, who forbids to make a picture. . . . The miracle is, to me, that all these people who might have forgotten, for years, that they are Jews, suddenly facing death, remember who they are. And this seems to me a great thing."

of injustice. He will certainly be more irritable when he sees a photo of cudgeling South African policemen or American sheriffs setting howling dogs on black civil rights activists. Evidently, the fact that I have come to find life as a human being difficult has not turned me into a brute.

After all, ultimately, all that distinguishes me from the people among whom I live is a fluctuating sense of unease, which is sometimes more and sometimes less pronounced. This unease is *social* and not metaphysical in kind. It is not being or nothingness or God or his absence that unsettles me; it is society. It and it alone has caused the existential vertigo in the face of which I am seeking to assert my upright gait. It and it alone has robbed me of my trust in the world. Metaphysical angst is a concern of the highest standing, and those who have always known who and what they are, and why, and that they will always be permitted to continue being who and what they are may continue to address it. That it is their preserve is not what makes me feel wretched when I compare myself to them.

In my unrelenting quest to explore the basic condition of being a victim and my confrontation both with the obligation to be a Jew and the impossibility of doing so, my experience has led me to the conclusion that the most extreme impositions and demands placed on us are of a physical and social kind. I appreciate that this experience has rendered me incapable of profound and lofty speculation. My hope is that it might have placed me in a better position to comprehend reality.

2 Between Vietnam and Israel: The Dilemma of Political Commitment (1967)

As COINCIDENCE WOULD have it, a couple of weeks ago, the author of this contribution had the opportunity to speak within a few days of each other with the German writers Alfred Andersch[24] and Rolf Schroers[25] about the political commitment of the intellectual. Implicitly, they were all more or less in agreement that this commitment could only be, in the widest sense of the word and however problematically so, *leftist* in nature. The former officer Schroers, temperamentally a conservative and a member of the FDP,[26] albeit on the left of the party; the former young communist Andersch; and the leftist, in every sense of the word homeless author of these lines—in keeping with the tradition, which has prevailed since the Dreyfus Affair, it went without saying for all three of them that an intellectual who becomes politically active by definition does so on the *left*, where, to quote Alfred Polgar, "the heart of humanity beats."[27] Beyond this tacit agreement, however, certain problems presented themselves. Did an intellectual not give up his political freedom by associating himself all too closely with political events? Did he not limit his ability to adhere to the crucial virtue of tolerance by committing himself? Was it permissible to judge every domestic German problem from a leftist position and to use each and every barely appropriate opportunity to take to the stage and speak out? What happened to the authorial dignity of, say, Günter Grass as he traversed the German lands in his role as the bard of the SPD?[28] Did the intellectual not jeopardize his authority and diminish the impact of his words by signing an endless stream of protest telegrams and manifestos?

---

24 Alfred Andersch (1914–1980) served as a Communist official in 1932–1933 and was imprisoned in Dachau for six months in 1933. Called up in 1943, he deserted in 1944. After the war, he became one of the most influential West German writers. He moved to Switzerland in 1958.

25 Rolf Schroers (1919–1982) was a Nazi officer during the Second World War and later became a successful German writer. He played a vital role in the FDP and stood for election to parliament.

26 FDP is the acronym for the liberal Free Democratic Party, founded in 1948. In the 1950s, the party opposed the denazification process and swelled its ranks with numerous former Nazis (including SS members).

27 Polgar made this remark in a piece on Georges de la Fouchardière published in *Schwarz auf Weiss* (Berlin: Rowohlt, 1929), 283–88.

28 SPD is the acronym for the center-left Social Democratic Party of Germany, initially founded in 1863.

The discussions did not lead to any definite conclusion. I, for my part—to introduce, under stylistic and moral duress, the personal pronoun one ordinarily likes to hide behind bashful circumlocution and feigned detachment and objectivity—I, then, for my part, in the face of my interlocutors' reservations, argued with some passion *for* the merits of political commitment.

The concerns regarding the authority of the author, his "aura," were not really that important, I suggested. Even the "beauty" of the more or less beautiful words with which the writers enchanted their readers one should not take all too seriously. Nor, as one could deduce from Herbert Marcuse's magnificent essay "Repressive Tolerance," did tolerance constitute an absolute historical or moral value. Sartre's activities were a case in point. Not only did he not fear a loss of authority should he speak out, even the possibility that he might make a fool of himself did not deter him. There were always plausible and obvious priorities, and one of them was the commitment to a cause, which might not be a genuine good cause yet but would, as opposed to others, seem to have the potential of one day becoming one.

The proponent of left-leaning commitment had no great difficulties in arguing the case he was inclined, and felt enjoined, to make. He referred to Vietnam. There, a small people was being crushed by the world's strongest military machine. In no way could one suggest that a symmetry existed between the atrocities perpetrated by either side as though both were equally guilty. Or one might think of Greece, he pointed out, where the new order and the new morality were on the march. Yet come the holiday season next summer, few archaeologically interested cultural tourists would give it a miss. Or of Bolivia. There one had apparently already tortured the young French philosopher Régis Debray, a dazzling human being of stirring physical and intellectual prowess, half to death, and it is still a distinct possibility that he might be executed, regardless of what the general who was his president thought.[29] Actually, he added, Régis Debray's case gave a fairly clear indication of the meaningful nature of political commitment, which always came into its own at the point at which the committed intellectual was able to bring his actions into full agreement with his words, when he was physically engaged in the implementation of the goals he had spoken and written about.

Nor did this commitment in any way contradict the protest that had to be raised against the despicable treatment of men like the Soviet writers Daniel and Sinyavsky.[30] After all, they and their afflicted peers in the countries of the social-

---

29 In the event, Debray was released in December 1970.

30 Yuli Markovich Daniel (1925–1988) and Andrei Donatovich Sinyavsky (1925–1997) were arrested in September 1965 and tried and convicted the following year for anti-Soviet propaganda. Their case caused considerable international consternation. Following their release in 1970 and 1971, respectively, Daniel worked as a translator in the Soviet Union while Sinyavsky moved to Paris in 1973, where he subsequently held a chair at the Sorbonne.

ist bloc saw themselves as being engaged in leftist oppositional activity targeting a right-wing, reactionary orthodoxy. Their misfortune only underscored further that the intellect continues to stand on the left while the might, which is evil even when it tries to be good and despite being rooted in a theory predicated on right and justice, is located squarely on the political right.

All other things being even, given that U Thant saw the world being propelled straight into the Third World War in Vietnam, one should always look to Vietnam to gain a sense of direction.[31] What that direction should be was a matter of dispute; indeed, this was an irreconcilably contested issue. Yet no one could opt for agreeable "objectivity" in the matter.

The situation was this straightforward. From the perspective of the intellectual interested in political commitment, the current political situation really did cut such an overly obvious figure. One could not but give the *terrible simplificateur*,[32] overcoming all fear of mockery, for the horrors of the world were indeed this straightforward.

Yet then something transpired that, for the author who is telling the truth about himself in this article and for thousands of others who are of like mind, transformed the horrific simplicity of the political landscape into an even more horrifying complicacy. The Arab states, supported by the Soviet Union and the entire socialist bloc, seemed to be on the verge of snuffing out the tiny state of Israel.

Against this backdrop, Claude Lanzmann, a member of the Sartre "family" who accompanied Sartre and Simone de Beauvoir on their recent trip to Egypt and Israel, declared that, as a socialist and Marxist, he was now compelled to nail his flag unreservedly to the mast of this state, which, in the parlance of the socialist bloc, is a bridgehead of American imperialism in the Middle East. He regretted, Lanzmann added, that he had not professed this unambiguous commitment sooner. What had happened to Sartre's student and friend had likewise happened to the author of this contribution, on whom Sartre has had a greater formative influence than any other philosopher; and it surely must have happened to innumerable other people too, who, by opting for Vietnam's cause, had opted for themselves, ranging from Jewish leftists of some obscure socialist denomination to, maybe, Howard Levy,[33] the Jewish colonel and physician who refused to instruct US recruits destined for Vietnam because, "as a man of Jewish extraction," he did not want to serve the Hitler fan Marshall Ky.[34]

---

31 The Burmese politician and diplomat U Thant (1909–1974) was the third secretary general of the United Nations (1962–1971).

32 Translation: terrible simplifier.

33 In 1967, US Army captain Howard Levy was imprisoned for refusing to train Special Forces soldiers for Vietnam.

34 Nguyen Cao Ky (1930–2011) was chief of the South Vietnam Air Force and later became prime minister of South Vietnam from 1965 to 1967.

Only weeks before this event, I had still been able to see myself in a straight-forward way as one of those leftist intellectuals who, in a manner tempered by their critical habitus and self-mockery, indulge the revulsion of some while offering a measure of gratification to themselves and others. I recall participating in the Nuremberg Colloquy, which took place in April 1967.[35] There, a young German wearing a traditional jacket à la Heidegger, who was so enraged that all the blood had drained from his face, made it known that, in the fullness of time, one would know where to find figures like me. I can still sense the childlike pride that took hold of me in that moment, given that even for the likes of me one's political commitment was evidently no longer an entirely empty gesture and one could console oneself with the thought that it entailed at least a minimum of risk. Yet the massing of Arab troops on all of Israel's borders cut off, had to cut off, the partly self-righteous and in any case intellectually not exactly well-founded gratification drawn from this form of political commitment, which one used to call "antifascist."

Leaving to one side all the obviously nonsensical possible points of comparison, what set me apart from Sartre in this situation, or from Enzensberger and all the other committed leftist intellectuals for whom the existence of the state of Israel is a "cause," to be sure, but not one that concerns their own place in the world?[36] Worlds set us apart. Regardless of whether we are entirely of Jewish extraction or not, whether we are religious or totally assimilated atheists, now that Israel is under threat, those of us who have been compelled to recognize that we bear the Jewish lot have been expelled from the community of which we were a part only yesterday. Those of us who belong to the generation that experienced Hitler's crimes in the flesh find ourselves as isolated, once again, as we were between 1933 and 1945. We no longer have a choice, can no longer choose *ourselves*, because we have already been chosen: as victims. And there is some likelihood that we will once more have to play the role that was thrust on us back then.

The singular and irreducible core of the Jewish condition is now becoming clear: it is the inescapability of being a Jew, a state one can only accept and whose implications are ineluctable. One may want to be a leftist intellectual one day but no longer the next. This is almost entirely a matter of free will. Being a Jew, by contrast, and I repeat: regardless of whether one is a religious Jew, entirely of Jewish extraction, or, in "racial" terms, of mixed descent, is a priori not a matter of choice. The Jew is compelled to stay who he is and must accept that it is so. And this will also determine his stance on the looming Israeli-Arab conflict.

---

35 The Nuremberg Colloquies (Nürnberger Gespräche), initiated by Nuremberg's municipal head of cultural affairs, Hermann Glaser (a Social Democrat), took place between 1965 and 1969 and drew fierce right-wing criticism. At the first colloquy in 1965, Fritz Bauer discussed the relevance of Auschwitz, inter alia, with H. G. Adler.

36 Hans Magnus Enzensberger (born 1929) is an extremely influential and well-connected (formerly West) German literary figure.

I have before me the text of an appeal issued by leftist French intellectuals calling for peace in the Middle East. It refers to the friendship between the signatories and the Arab people and emphatically rejects American imperialism. It then expressly pleads Israel's case. The security and sovereignty of the state, including its freedom of shipping, needed to be protected. Peace should be achieved in direct negotiations between the nations concerned and serve their peoples. The appeal is well-meaning and seeks to do justice to all parties. Since it is abundantly clear that the Arab states do not wish to negotiate and are under no circumstances minded to acknowledge Israel's right to exist, the appeal is also entirely theoretical in nature. That Sartre, Simone de Beauvoir, Claude Roy, Jean Cassou, Abbé Morel, and Pastor Westphal signed the document is understandable and should be countenanced, the lack of realism on the part of its authors reflected in the text notwithstanding.[37] After all, given that their existence is not at stake, non-Jewish intellectuals can afford to reaffirm their political and moral principles in this situation. However, that the Jews Laurent Schwartz, Vladimir Jankélévitch, and Clara Malraux-Goldschmidt also put their names to the writ takes us into the realm of a tragic kind of irony.[38] They are cleaving to principles that have become self-contradictory and that reality has rendered obsolete.

What is the point of professing one's friendship with the Arab people when they are quite obviously not interested in this declaration of love und would quite unceremoniously treat the philosopher Jankélévitch, the mathematician Schwartz, and the writer Clara Malraux in an extremely inclement manner, given half a chance? What is the point, in this context, of condemning American imperialism? To be sure, it exists, or, to be more precise, America absolutely is pursuing a policy of belligerent violence in Vietnam, but this has nothing to do with the crisis in the Middle East, where it is, after all, not the Americans who are threatening to wipe out a small country.

---

37 Claude Roy (1915–1997) was a writer, journalist, and translator who joined the Communist Party during the Second World War. Having reported on events in Hungary in 1956, he subsequently moved away from Communism. He opposed the war in Algeria and was one of the signatories of the *Manifesto of the 121*. Jean Cassou (1897–1986) was a writer and art historian who fought in the resistance and was imprisoned by the Vichy regime. From 1945 to 1965, he was the director of the National Museum of Modern Art. Jankélévitch was his brother-in-law. Abbé Maurice Morel (1908–1991) was (alongside his priesthood) an abstract painter and stained glass artist. Charles Westphal (1896–1972) was a leading French Calvinist and played a prominent role in shaping his denomination's attitudes toward Jewish-Christian relations.

38 Laurent-Moïse Schwartz (1915–2002) was a mathematician and recipient of the Fields Medal (1950). Not least following the "disappearance" of his graduate student Maurice Audin in Algiers in 1957, Schwartz became a vocal opponent of the war in Algeria and was temporarily suspended from his professorship at the École Polytechnique because he had signed the *Manifesto of the 121*. Clara Malraux, née Goldschmidt, (1897–1982) was a writer, translator (inter alia, of Virginia Woolf, Franz Kafka, and Siegfried Kracauer), and memoirist. She was the first wife of André Malraux (they divorced during the war).

It would seem that the leftist Jewish intellectuals have not yet grasped fully that in the face of what is occurring on Israel's borders, their leftist comportment becomes meaningless. They are in for a rude awakening when they are confronted with the incontrovertible fact that they are in no position to choose or take a stance because they have already been chosen and put in their place. Why so?

Well, the matter is straightforward enough: for every single Jew the world over, whatever his political orientation, whether he is an intellectual or a businessman or a craftsman, the existence of the small Jewish state is an "existential" issue because not only have the Jews in Israel, to use a formulation Ernst Bloch coined in another context, themselves acquired the "upright gait," they have also taught the Jews who live in the diaspora and may have no intention of ever going to Israel, not even on holiday, how to adopt a firm step and straight posture.

The state of Israel has so resoundingly disproved the most stupid antisemitic legends—that the Jews were cowards, that they knew what to do with a bank note but not how to operate a plow, that they were incapable of forming a state—that even the most dogged old Nazi or neo-Nazi no longer dares repeat them. Every Jew, no matter where he lives, lives off this achievement. Even if he has long since constituted himself as wholly French or wholly American, it gives him a proper place in the world, whether he admits this to himself or not. Thus, the leftist Jewish intellectual is enlisted *by*, and turned over *to*, his lot. He has not freely elected his commitment; it has been thrust on him under inescapable duress. Since hostile armies have massed around Israel, since the most forthright voices in the Arab lands have let it be known that the small country should be turned into a large concentration camp, since there is talk of driving the Israelis into the sea, he is no longer a leftist intellectual but merely a Jew. For Auschwitz lies behind him, and the hoped-for Auschwitz II on the Mediterranean may well lie ahead of his brethren from whom he cannot remove himself because the world will not let him.

As it has done once before, the Jewish *condition humaine* has, by tragic means, relieved the Jew of this choice. Which is not to deny that, as a leftist, he is faced with an awful dilemma. After all, the conflict in Vietnam goes on, the escalation has not been halted, Vietnam's plight is real and continues to demand the solidarity of leftist Jews, and this even though Hanoi has assured Nasser by telegram of its unreserved approval. How can one escape this dilemma?

One can simplify the matter by constructing a hypothetical case, asking what would follow if both General Giap and Itzhak Rabin in his capacity as chief of staff were to begin recruiting volunteers and forming international brigades.[39] Where, then, should a young leftist Jew who is fit for military service head? This may look like something of a conundrum, yet assuming the young person presented with

---

39 Vo Nguyen Giap (1912–2013) was the North Vietnamese deputy prime minister, minister of defense, and commander in chief.

this choice wants to opt for *authenticity,* its solution is in fact predetermined. For the author of this contribution, this issue is already settled. His age and physical constitution allowing, he would place himself at Rabin's disposal and "betray" General Giap, even if this did bring with it the risk of suddenly finding himself fighting, while under Israeli command, side by side with an American marine who may well have been involved in the awful combat in Vietnam only a moment ago and who might even be a segregationist and antisemite back home in South Carolina.

The dilemma of the leftist Jewish intellectual is purely psychological in nature. Objectively, his conduct is already predetermined. In other words, once again, he is not *free,* no more so than the author of these lines was when, in 1941, he joined the resistance. After all, even if he had been "loyal" to the German occupation authorities, he would still have been deported. Consequently, he is intellectually no longer interested in resolving the conundrums of political commitment. As long as Israel, and he himself and his arduously acquired upright gait with it, are under threat, the problem as such is of no concern to him. He has been yanked from his community of convictions and, regardless of his own wishes, he has been compulsorily thrust into the community of the persecuted. If he is reluctant to admit this to himself, he need only imagine what would ensue if Israel were decisively defeated. Hundreds of thousands of Jews would pour out into the world. Yet again, a Jewish problem of an entirely different order of magnitude would exist, and the signatories of the aforementioned appeal, for all their illusory freedom, might well count themselves lucky just to stay alive.

The politically committed Jew who is concerned about the situation in Vietnam and Greece herewith hands in his resignation, at least provisionally. He is being replaced by a Jew who has been exposed to the ultimate catastrophe. Will he regain his freedom and be able fully to resume his leftist commitment? This may depend not least on the extent to which he is able to sustain his authenticity in the days that lie ahead.

3 Virtuous Antisemitism (1969)

WHEN DE GAULLE was toppled, quite a few people felt as gloomy as Heine's two grenadiers did when they heard of Napoleon's detention;[40] and so, indeed, did I. Yet in New York, alas, the French UN delegate Armand Bérard had nothing better to do (according to the *Nouvel Observateur* of March 5) than to cry out despairingly, "*C'est l'or juif!*"[41] And no disclaimer followed. On the political right, on the political left, everything is reversed. Antisemitism has this ability and, as Stefan George once put it, "It sweeps into the ring."[42]

Classical antisemitism is taking on a contemporaneous guise. Yet its previous guise too lives on: a rare case of genuine coexistence. The past stays with us and will continue to stay with us in the form of the crooked-nosed and bowlegged Jew forced to flee by one circumstance or another or, rather, by them all. This is also how you will see him on Arab propaganda placards and pamphlet covers, which I gather formerly brown gentlemen whose first language is German help produce, now hidden carefully behind Arabic names. The relevant new notions reared their head in the immediate aftermath of the Six-Day War and are gradually gaining ground. They hinge on the Israeli oppressor trampling peaceable Palestinian land underfoot with the iron tread of Roman legions. Today's anti-Israelism and anti-Zionism and the antisemitism of yesteryear find themselves in absolute agreement. Apparently, one can seamlessly merge the notion of the Jew as the oppressive legionary with the iron tread with that of the Jew as the runaway with the bowed legs. How the images finally resemble each other!

What certainly is new, however, is that this form of antisemitism, now dressed up as anti-Israelism, is located firmly on the left. Whereas in the past it was considered the socialism of fools, it is now evolving into an integrative constituent of socialism per se, and the socialists, of their own free volition, are universally turning themselves into fools.

---

40 This is a reference to Heinrich Heine's poem "The Grenadiers" (1822) about two soldiers returning to France from Russian captivity after Napoleon's defeat.

41 Translation: "It's the Jewish gold!"

42 This is a reference to the final line of the poem beginning with the line (in Richard F. C. Hull's translation) "Call it the bolt that struck the sign that led" ["*Nennt es den blitz der traf den wink der lenkte*"] in Stefan George's *Star of the Covenant* (1914). The line actually reads, "I guide toward dance I sweep into the ring." The first-person narrator is the god who forcefully facilitates the creation of the exclusive spiritual realm envisaged by George. Améry evidently felt that this imagery was well suited to reflect the ability of antisemitism to unite otherwise disparate, indeed, even mutually attenuating or contradictory forces. For Hull's translation of the poem, see Georg Peter Landmann (ed.), *Stefan George in fremden Sprachen* (Düsseldorf and Munich: Helmut Küpper, 1973), 480.

For an instructive account of this development, one can turn to Givet's *La Gauche contre Israel*,[43] published by Pauvert more than a year ago. Or one might simply take note of certain landmark occurrences. One might read the report "The Third Front" in the journal *konkret*, for example.[44] One of its section headings reads, "Is Israel a Police State?" The question is purely rhetorical. Needless to say, Israel is just that. Not to mention napalm, the blowing up of the houses of peaceable Arab peasants, and the pogroms against Arabs in the streets of Jerusalem. One knows one's stuff: the situation there is just like the one in Vietnam or previously in Algeria. In his new role as the terror-spreading Goliath, the bow-legged runaway is apparently an absolute natural.

I do mean *the* left and by no means merely the still more or less orthodox communist parties in the West or the policies of the ("real-existing") socialist states. For the latter, anti-Israelism, grafted on to the traditional antisemitism of the Slav peoples, is simply part and parcel of their strategic and tactical response to a specific constellation. The stars do not lie, and the Gomulkas of this world know what they can expect.[45] *C'est de bonne guerre!*[46] What more is there to say?

Far more disconcerting is the fact that the intellectual left affiliated with no political party has appropriated this imagery. For years, to take the German case, one celebrated the armed Israelis and, not least, the stylish girls in uniform, tilling the Israeli soil. Obvious feelings of guilt were thus discharged in a tainted currency, which was always going to become tiresome. Fortunately, for once, the Jew, instead of being burned,[47] has now emerged as the imperious victor and occupying power, which brings us back to napalm and all that. The country breathed a sigh of relief. Everyone now felt able to express themselves in the manner of the *Deutsche National- und Soldaten-Zeitung*,[48] and even those on the left were empowered to enforce their jargon of commitment as though its validity were self-evident.

This much is for sure: antisemitism resides in anti-Israelism and anti-Zionism as the thunderstorm does in the cloud, and it has become respectable again. In its vulgar guise, it can freely speak of the "criminal state of Israel"; in its more genteel

---

43 Jacques Givet, *La Gauche contre Israël? Essai sur le néo-antisémitisme* [The Left against Israel? Essay on the New Antisemitism] (Paris: Pauvert, 1968).

44 Detlef Schneider, "Die dritte Front," in *konkret* no. 7 (1969): 28–33 and no. 8 (1969): 26–33.

45 As head of the Polish Communist Party and de facto head of state, Władysław Gomułka (1905–1982) oversaw the massive wave of repression against the country's Jews following the Six-Day War, which led to a massive exodus of Polish Jews.

46 Translation: "All's fair in love and war!"

47 This is presumably a reference to Gotthold Ephraim Lessing's *Nathan the Wise* (1779). In act 4, scene 2, the Patriarch three times dismisses mitigating circumstances presented by the Templar with the words, "It matters not, the Jew must still be burned."

48 The *Deutsche National- und Soldaten-Zeitung* is a far-right German weekly established in 1951.

guise, it is at liberty to describe Israel as the "bridgehead of imperialism" while lamenting in passing the ill-conceived sense of solidarity that ties more or less all Jews, a few laudable exceptions apart, to the tiny state and expressing outrage at the fact that the Parisian Baron Rothschild thinks French Jewry should pay a levy to support Israel.

Invariably, antisemitism has an easy ride. The emotional infrastructure is in place, and by no means just in Poland or Hungary. The antisemite enjoys "demythologizing" the Jewish pioneer state. It strikes him that capitalism, in the form of the Jewish plutocracy, was behind the creation of this state from the outset. Not that he would explicitly mention this plutocracy. To do so would amount to a *lapsus linguae*.[49] Even so: *c'est l'or juif!* Surely nobody can be in any doubt about the actual character of a country born of a bad idea and established in a bad place, which has fought (and won) more than one bad war.

To avoid unnecessary misunderstandings: I know as well as the next man that Israel does indeed find itself in the disagreeable role of being an occupying power. I would not dream of countenancing everything that various Israeli governments do. My relations to this country, described by Thomas Mann in his Joseph tetralogy as "a Mediterranean land, not exactly like home, a bit dusty and stony," are virtually nonexistent.[50] I have never been there, I do not speak its language, how little I know of its culture borders on the embarrassing, and its religion is not mine. And yet, the existence of no other state means more to me. At this point, all descriptive or analytical objectivity ends, and commitment ceases to be merely some obligation entered into voluntarily and becomes, in various senses of the word, existential in nature.

Israel, the now fashionable anti-Israelism, the old-fashioned antisemitism that invariably creeps into every such new fashion—these are issues that for anyone who is in some way "affected" by them (i.e., Jews and persons classified as Jews by the Reich's Citizenship Law of September 15, 1935) are of existential subjective significance—and that may well, for this very reason, attain a degree of objectivity bordering on that of natural law. After all, even if, according to some perverted pseudo-Marxist theology, Israel may be beholden a hundred times over to the sinfulness of advanced technological development, even by the most straightforward, never mind more sophisticated, standards there can be no doubt that this pioneer country is the most endangered of all the states in its geopolitical region. It wins victory on victory and yet catastrophe continues to loom, and that catastrophe certainly cannot be avoided by walking straight into it (i.e., by seeing Israel incorporated into some Palestinian Federation).

---

49 Translation: "A slip of the tongue."
50 Thomas Mann, *Joseph and His Brothers*, trans. John E. Woods (New York: Knopf, 2005), 40. *Joseph and His Brothers* (1933–1943) is a four-part novel based on the biblical account of Joseph's life.

The day will come when the Arab states, whom I wish peace and good fortune, will catch up with Israel's developmental advantage, and demographic pressures will do the rest. Until then, until peace and progress in the economic and technological spheres have changed the Arabs' minds and allowed them to recognize Israel within secure borders, Israel must under all circumstances be preserved.

This is the actual issue. For whom? Here the subjective state of mind striving toward historical objectivity comes into its own. For Jews (Jews and persons classified as . . . and so on), for every single one of them, wherever they may live, Israel's continued existence is indispensable. "Am I going to be forced to call out 'long live Johnson!' if the United States is the only country to stand against the annihilation of Israel? I am prepared to do so," Claude Lanzmann, left-wing radical, writer, and one of Sartre's students, exclaimed on the eve of the Six-Day War. There you have somebody who knew what was at stake and what was required. For each and every Jew, whether he grasps this or not, is abandoned to a catastrophic fate, he is a "catastrophe Jew." The Black Panthers graffiti "Run, pale Jew" on the shops and residences of Jewish tradesmen in Harlem, flippantly oblivious to the long-standing bond that chained the Jew to the negro in the United States, a bond no bourgeois Jewish tradesman, no matter how sleazy, would ever have betrayed.

Who can guarantee that a future US administration will not one day feed the Jew to the negro in celebration of a grand day of atonement? Who can assure the influential and in some cases wealthy Jews of France that the heirs of the Drumont, Maurras, and Xavier Vallat will not one day become a virulent force again?[51] Who can vouch for the fact that Franz-Josef Strauß, once in power, would not dream up something suited to make even a certain newspaper tycoon think twice about making further sordid donations to an Israeli government sordidly willing to accept them?[52] Nobody guarantees nothing. This is no paranoid fantasy

---

51 Édouard Drumont (1844–1917) was one of the pioneers of modern political antisemitism. He was best known for his groundbreaking antisemitic treatise *La France juive* (1886). Charles Maurras (1868–1952), who came to prominence as a vocal anti-Dreyfusard, founded the far-right *Action Française* and later supported the Vichy regime. After the war, he received a life sentence but was released on medical grounds shortly before his death. Xavier Vallat (1891–1972) was profoundly shaped by the ideas of Drumont and Maurras and served in a number of positions within the Vichy regime, notably, in 1941–1942, as first director of the General Commissariat for Jewish Affairs. In this capacity, he laid some of the decisive groundwork for the implementation of the Shoah in France. Sentenced to ten years in prison after the war, he was released early and rejoined the far-right movement as a journalist and activist.

52 Franz-Josef Strauß (1915–1988) was a larger-than-life, staunchly conservative Bavarian politician firmly and emphatically on the right wing of the Christian Democratic movement in West Germany. He first joined the federal cabinet in 1953, serving as defense minister from 1956 to 1962 and as finance minister from 1966 to 1969. During his time in the defense ministry, his heavy-handed persecution of West Germany's foremost weekly, *Der Spiegel*, caused a major scandal and earned him considerable notoriety. The "newspaper tycoon" in question is Axel Cäsar Springer (1912–1985). Alongside serious papers like *Die Welt* and middlebrow papers

nor just a matter of the dangers invariably inherent in the human condition. The past, the most recent past, continues to burn.

Now all my leftist friends will tell me that I am joining the battalions exploiting the six (or let it be just five or four) million murdered Jews to blackmail public opinion. This is a risk worth taking. It is a smaller risk than the one my friends would have us take when they plead for the self-disbandment of the "Zionist" state of Israel.

Practical political reason dictates that Israel, indeed, that Israel in particular, deserves the solidarity of any left that is not intent on abrogating itself (and there is no reason why it should need to ignore the unbearable fate of the Arab refugees in order to honor this commitment). To be sure, it is a commitment less binding for the non-Jewish leftist than it is for Jews of any political stripe or none because one can resign from the left, whereas, as a pioneering antisemite like Lanz-Liebenfels already knew, nobody can leave their Jewishness behind. Even so, the left is predicated on an unwritten moral code, which it may not compromise. "Where there is a stronger party, always side with the weaker one"—how inviolable is the truth of this common place! And the stronger party—who could possibly claim otherwise?—are the Arabs. They are stronger in number, stronger in oil, stronger in dollars (one need only ask Aramco or Kuwait), and they definitely have the stronger prospects.

Yet clearly, the left is spellbound by the brave Palestinian partisans who are indeed poorer than Moshe Dayan's men.[53] It fails to recognize that, the Rothschilds and a prosperous Jewish American middle class notwithstanding, the Jew is still worse off than Frantz Fanon's colonized individual. It is as oblivious to this fact as it is to the anti-imperialist liberation struggle fought by the Jews against the British in Mandate Palestine. Nor, for that matter, are the Israelis responsible for the fact that the Soviet Union soon forgot what Gromyko had recited with beautiful vibrato before the UN in 1948:

> As regards the Jewish State, its existence is already a fact; whether or not anyone likes that State, it is actually there. . . . The USSR delegation cannot but express surprise at the position adopted by the Arab States in the Palestine question, and particularly at the fact those States—or some of them, at least—have

---

like the *Berliner Morgenpost* and the *Hamburger Abendblatt*, he owned a number of extremely successful tabloids (*Bild*, *B.Z.*). Especially in 1968, his enterprise became the object of violent protests because many of the protesting students and activists held his papers responsible for creating the hostile environment that, inter alia, had facilitated the attempt on the life of the prominent activist Rudi Dutschke. In 1972, the Red Army Faction carried out a bomb attack on his publishing firm's headquarters in Hamburg. Axel Springer was a staunch supporter of Israel.

53 Moshe Dayan (1915–1981) was one of Israel's leading military commanders but also served as a deputy in the Knesset and minister in various governments. He was highly praised for his role in the wars of 1956 and 1967, but many later blamed him for Israel's lack of preparedness in 1973. Instantly recognizable not least due to his eye patch (he had lost an eye fighting against Vichy France in Syria during the Second World War), for many in the West he embodied the Israeli military.

resorted to such action as sending their troops into Palestine and carrying out military operations aimed at the suppression of the national liberation movement in Palestine. . . . We cannot identify the vital interests of the peoples of the Arab East with the statements of certain Arab leaders or with those actions of the Governments of certain Arab States which we are witnessing at present.[54]

As I say, this was the position of the Soviet Union, a superpower engaged in superpower politics. In the long run, the Soviets were presumably unable to ignore the fact that there are more Arabs than Jews, that there is more Arab than Israeli oil, that military bases in Arab states have greater strategic value than a foothold in Israel. The left in the wider and widest sense, however, and especially the protesting radical left with whom, in many respects, I feel connected, cannot take recourse to this superpower excuse.

If it heeds the law presiding at its birth, the left is obligated to understand: to grasp the tragic weakness of the Jewish state and of every individual Jew in the diaspora, to understand what lies behind the façade of the bourgeois Jewish middle class, behind the myth of the moneylending and fabulously wealthy Jew (from Jud Süß to the current Rothschilds and a handful of Jewish Hollywood moguls).[55] Jews handle capital with some regularity, but they have never controlled it. To this day, they no more call the shots on Wall Street than they were in charge of the heavy industry in Imperial Germany.

Israel is no more a bulwark of capitalism now than it was when the first pioneers began to dig the soil there. Nor can the Arab states reasonably be considered progressive. The left, alas, closes its eyes. As coincidence would have it, I recently stumbled across a text by Hans Blüher in which he writes, "A genuine history of Europe should be written not as it has in the past, the Jew featuring here and there anecdotally. . . . Rather, the account should render the consistent might of Jewry as

---

54 UN Security Council, 299th Meeting, May 21, 1948, *Official Records: Third Year*, no. 71, 6–8. https://digitallibrary.un.org/record/636336/files/S_PV-299-EN.pdf. Andrei Gromyko (1909–1989) was the Soviet foreign minister from 1957 to 1985.

55 Joseph Süß Oppenheimer (1698–1738), called "Jud Süß" by his detractors, was a tax collector and leading financier at the court of the principality of Württemberg who antagonized the nobility by modernizing the territory's tax system to the advantage of the ducal exchequer. Oppenheimer was arrested within hours of the death of his patron, Duke Karl Alexander. Following a show trial, he was executed (by strangulation) and his corpse put on public display for six weeks. Oppenheimer has frequently been seen as *the* paradigmatic "court Jew" and features in numerous literary works, including Lion Feuchtwanger's novel *Jud Süß* (1925), which, in turn, was cannibalized by Veit Harlan for the script of the infamous Nazi propaganda film of the same name (1940).

56 As a young man, the cultural historian and sexual theorist Hans Blüher (1888–1955) was a theoretician (and practitioner) of what he considered the homoerotic essence of the so-called Youth Movement that enthusiastically embraced a romanticizing, vitalist love of nature in opposition to the ostensible decadence of urban civilization and industrial society. Following his conversion to heterosexuality and marriage, he became an increasingly outspoken *völkisch* antisemite.

a clandestine, constantly active imperious power visible."[56] One might just as well find this text verbatim in one of the numerous pseudointellectual Arab publications currently flooding the press. Likewise, Blüher—or, since antisemitism invariably levels intellectual distinctions, Streicher, for that matter—could be the author of the remarks the education minister of the progressive state of Syria recently addressed to the director general of UNESCO: "The hatred which we indoctrinate into the minds of our children from their birth is sacred."[57] All this would barely merit attention, and Blüher in all his craziness could enjoy the restful peace of oblivion, had the intellectual left in Western Europe not appropriated this lexicon and accepted the norms it conveys.

It would seem that a new notion of Jewish guilt is being construed from the historical calamity of the "Jewish Question" (in reality: the antisemites' question), a calamity of which the establishment of the now real-existing state of Israel may well be a part. The responsibility for this development lies squarely with a left that has lost its sense of self. As Robert Misrahi, a French philosopher who, like the aforementioned Claude Lanzmann, belongs to Sartre's extended family, recently stated, "Anti-Zionism is a fundamentally reactionary phenomenon camouflaged by its revolutionary and anti-colonial rhetoric about Israel."

The time has come for a revision and renewed intellectual self-renunciation on the left. For it is the left that is providing antisemitism with a nefarious dialectical veneer of virtuousness. The alliance between the antisemitic philistines' coven and the leftists on the barricades is, to use the language imposed by this issue, contrary to nature; it is a sin against the spirit.[58] The likes of the Polish general Moczar may be able to get away with the transmutation of crude antisemitism into contemporaneous anti-Israelism.[59] The left has to be more truthful. There is no such thing as virtuous antisemitism. How did Sartre put it many years ago in *Anti-Semite and Jew*? "What the antisemite wishes, what he prepares, is the death of the Jew."[60]

---

57 The letter from Suleiman al-Khash to René Maheu was publicized in the Baathist paper *Al Thawra* on May 3, 1968.
58 The expression "philistines' coven" is used here for "Spießer-Stammtisch." A *Stammtisch* is a table in a pub reserved for a specific round of regular guests. The term can be used in a neutral, descriptive sense but also has rather more sinister and exclusionary connotations. The online version of the *Duden*, which records the current standard use of German, defines *Stammtischpolitik* (i.e., *Stammtisch* politics) as "naïve political discussion; talking politics at the *Stammtisch* in an unqualified, unobjective manner."
59 As Poland's minister of the interior from 1964 to 1968, General Mieczysław Moczar (1913–1986) was one of the leaders of the antisemitic campaign following the Six-Day War. He was also responsible for the crushing of the student protests in the late 1960s.
60 Jean-Paul Sartre, *Anti-Semite and Jew* (New York: Schocken, 1948), 49.

4 The New Left's Approach to "Zionism" (1969)

I︲ᴛʜɪs ᴄᴏɴᴛᴇxᴛ, unsightly as it may be, the word *Zionism* simply cannot do without the quotation marks, even in the title, because the left—by which I mean the New Left, for the Old Left seems to be pretty much at a loss as to how to deal with this entire issue—has managed to de-define, if the expression be permitted, the actual concept of Zionism. Whom does this New Left consider a "Zionist"? In the first instance, there are obviously more or less all the inhabitants of the state of Israel, with the exception of a handful of tiny sects who, while living in and because of the political entity that is Israel, fight it—be it, like Uri Avnery, in the name of a "semitic region," or in the name of some global revolutionary dream. Yet for the New Left, all those diaspora Jews who care about the continued existence of the Israeli state (and I personally know none who do not sympathize with this country), are also Zionists, be they Baron Guy de Rothschild, an obscure Jewish community official, a concentration camp survivor, or a Soviet Jew who would emigrate to Israel if only one would let him. In short: for the New Left, Zionism is roughly what, in Germany, some thirty years ago was called "World Jewry." Leftist purism, leftist zeal, and leftist virtuousness (in Robespierre's sense) remonstrate against this Zionism, which leftists also like to call "National Zionism" in order to align it phonetically with National Socialism. In Israel the left sees the aggressor and oppressor, the armourbearer of Western, American imperialist oppression. In the Israeli army it sees an "army with a state," a formulation once used to describe the Prussian military. When it looks at Israel, it sees the ugly traits of militarism, if not of fascist violence. As a matter of course, its sympathies go out to the Arab Freikorps, especially the El Fatah. For the left, he bears the steely and transfigured face of the resistance fighter.

How, one wonders, did it come to this? What did it take for the global left (I repeat: for the purposes of this discussion, by left I mean the New Left) to embrace a hatred of Israel that, if left to run its course, of this much I am sure, can only serve the evil and unjust scourge of antisemitism? How did Marxist dialectical thought come to lend itself to the preparation of the coming genocide?

All this raises more questions than I can treat here, and the answers I offer can only be rough and approximate. In the first instance, one needs to address an issue that hitherto has not received sufficient attention because, for our leftist interlocutors, it is a conceptual taboo: the generational problem. Those of us who belong to the Old Left should not forget that the New Left is not only new in theoretical terms; it is also *young*. Those active in the New Left tend to be somewhere between eighteen and twenty-eight years of age. For them, the Nazi catastrophe is truly history, an event tailing off into some historical twilight zone and just as distant as, say, the French Revolution. Not that the young leftists do not know about Nazism. After all, in historical terms they also know about the French Revolution. In their struggle against the NPD,[61] they have demonstrated clearly and in the most gratifying manner that they are willing to stand by their convictions when the danger of fascism rears its head. And yet, they are oblivious to a number of phenomena specific to German National Socialism, which the concept of fascism fails to encapsulate. The firestorm unleashed on the Jews between 1939 and 1945 in particular they know about only from hearsay. They were not there when the neighbor, Mr. Schlesinger, was taken from his apartment, along with his family, and brought somewhere unpleasant. They did not attend the Allied occupation forces' screenings, in 1945, of films showing "German atrocities." They entered a world that, as they saw it, offered them a clean slate, and their conscience is clear. This allows them to understand "Nazi fascism" by *mis*understanding it. They are separated from it by a shock-absorbing historical space filled with illustrated broadsheets on which General Dayan may indeed look just like Field Marshall Kesselring.[62]

Yet one cannot understand the phenomenon of Israel without being fully cognizant of the Jewish catastrophe. Metaphorically speaking, everyone in Israel is the son or grandson of somebody who was gassed. By contrast, in Germany, and in the rest of Europe, one can take the liberty of being neither a "son" nor a "grandson." For the New Left, every hour is the zero hour, every day a new beginning. Yet the Jews, to use Hofmannsthal's words, can "never cast from their eyelids the lassitudes of long-forgotten peoples,"[63] neither in Israel nor elsewhere. Every Jew is, and will continue to be for a long time to come, on one of those death marches the evacuated Jewish concentration camp inmates were forced to undertake in the spring of 1945. The New Left does not understand that Israel can still be understood only against this bleak backdrop and that it will continue to be this way for some decades to come. How can one impress on the young that Israel is no country like any other? It is a sanctuary for deeply exhausted survivors and victims of persecution.

Fair enough, I hear people object, but of what concern is this to the Palestinian Arabs who have themselves been expelled from their house and home even

---

61 NPD is the acronym for the far right National Democratic Party of Germany, founded in 1964.
62 Albert Kesselring (1885–1960) was a highly decorated field marshal of the Luftwaffe, the aerial warfare branch of the German Wehrmacht during World War II. He commanded air forces in the invasions of Poland and France, the Battle of Britain, and the invasion of the Soviet Union.
63 This is a quotation (in the translation of Vernon Watkins) from Hugo von Hofmannsthal's well-known poem "Manche freilich" (Many truly; 1896).

though they were not the ones who killed the Jews by the million? This question, as a point of argument, is indeed difficult to answer. Should one point out that the Arab refugees, with a modicum of goodwill on the part of the Arab states, could have found refuge there, while all doors were closed to the Jews whom Hitler persecuted and threatened with murder? This is not a particularly strong or compelling response, I know. Yet, even if one allows for the consideration that Palestine may not have been the right place for the establishment of a Jewish state, the fact remains that the state of Israel now exists. It was created with just as much legitimacy under international law as any other. One cannot deliver the human beings who now live in this state to opponents who would clearly take no prisoners, no matter what the Arab propaganda abroad may claim.

Which brings us to the tragedy of Israeli aggression. To deny it would be simply nonsensical. Yes: Israel attacked first, both in the Suez campaign and in the Six-Day War. In the Gaza Strip, on the West Bank and the Sinai Peninsula, Israel is the occupying power—bringing with it all that being an occupying power implies. That an occupier, *any* occupier, is invariably also an oppressor goes without saying. To be sure, according to the unanimous testimony of more or less the entire world press, Israel operates in a relatively humane manner in the territories it has occupied, but she cannot escape the fundamental mechanism of violence and counterviolence. Arab guerrillas throw bombs, Israeli soldiers and policemen arrest, destroy structures with explosives, and expel. Even so, the question must surely be permitted whether Israel, in the situation in which it found itself, could have done anything other than attack and occupy territory. This, however, is of no concern to the New Left. In a frightening act of crass oversimplification, the lines are clearly and irreversibly drawn in their mind: the Arab freedom fighter, on the one hand, is neatly pitted against the Israeli oppressor, on the other.

The simplifying taxonomy driving their ideas and activities has its roots in the *myth of the liberation struggle that is both social-revolutionary and national in character*. Lest I be misunderstood I hasten to add: I would not dream of dismissing the social-revolutionary national liberation struggle per se as a myth. In many locations the world over, it is an equally bitter and justified reality. When Ben Bella readied himself in 1954 to strike against French colonialism, he was by no means beholden to some mythical idea. (Whatever became of Ben Bella, I wonder, and why do we no longer see any of the *chefs historiques* of the Algerian Revolution?) Neither Frantz Fanon, the theoretician of national-revolutionary force, nor Régis Debray, who sacrificed his freedom to the revolution, nor, needless to say, Che Guevara or Ho Chi Minh are, or were, proponents of a myth. Violent revolution turns to myth only where, for good reasons, it cannot and will not take place: in West Berlin, Frankfurt, Cologne, Paris, Grenoble, and so on. Here, the armed rebellion in the name of human emancipation has become a petrified myth and aestheticized slogan. Given the integral role of the national-revolutionary insurrection in Young Leftist thought (or lack thereof), the enthusiasm of the New Left inevitably had to coalesce around the resistance of the Palestinian Arabs, thus igniting their animosity toward the Israeli "oppressor." Vietnam, the struggle of the Bolivian guerrillas, the resistance movement in Greece, the Black Panther movement, the El Fatah—they all suddenly became indistinguishable.

Am I suggesting that the *résistance* of the Fedayeen lacks all legitimacy?[64] Of course not. Those who sneak through the Israeli lines and, drawing on the rules of the *maquis*,[65] challenge a relatively powerful occupying power are not all blindly indoctrinated fanatics; some of them are brave men. Yet only those oblivious to history can refuse to recognize that the Israelis too are engaged in a struggle for national liberation and that this struggle is inordinately more dangerous and inordinately more tragic than that of the Palestinian Arabs. For here, sheer survival is at stake and the preservation of a shelter for the Jews of the diaspora who are just about still tolerated in the developed countries and would long since have perished under dramatic circumstances in the Arab states had they not been able to seek refuge in Israel. Israel is fighting for the life of each of her inhabitants. The Arabs, by contrast, are fighting for their territorial rights. There can surely be no doubt that a left that has not succumbed to myth should at least try not to pour oil into the fire in the form of its ill-thought-out anti-Israelism.

The young leftists will surely reject with disdain the suggestion that their anti-Zionism incorporates elements of crude antisemitism, and quite rightly so: I would not accuse any of those young people who do no more than boo or shout down an Israeli ambassador of personally nurturing antisemitic intentions. Yet, as our young would-be Marx experts should surely know, given the objective historical situation, individual intentions and goals as such count for little. The seedbed in which the Young Left operates with its anti-Zionist furor nurtures the sprouts of a centuries-old antisemitism, which has been anything but "mastered." Somewhere, every "Down with the Zionist oppression" finds an echo sounding remarkably like "Perish Judah!" The antisemitism aroused long ago, presumably by the fallacious notion of the deicide, is as virulent as ever in the collective subconscious of the European peoples. In the anti-Zionism of the Young Left it finds not only a well-functioning outlet but (supposedly) also an alibi. After all, the *Jews* have always had to play the bogeyman, the global foe. Little wonder, then, that they are once again being stigmatized as oppressors. Hence my contention that left-wing anti-Zionism must and will merge into the generalized antisemitism that is in the air, and which is in any case not without precedent on the left, unless the New Left repents at the eleventh hour, shakes off its guerrilla metaphysics, and finally, just for once, does what it constantly claims, on every suitable and unsuitable occasion, to be doing—namely, to "reflect" intellectually on a given situation.

---

64 Arab guerrillas operating especially in Israel and the Palestinian territories.
65 Guerrillas fighting in the French Résistance during World War II or against the Franco regime in Spain.

I would not want to draw my discussion to an inevitably premature close without pointing to one final and decisive fact. The anti-Zionism of the left is driving the overwhelming majority of the Jews in Europe and the United States who, with considerable justification, feel constantly endangered, into the arms of the reactionaries. Much as the Jews suffering under the official antisemitism of the states of the Warsaw Pact most likely—I have no reliable information on this issue at my disposal and can only speculate and infer—view the United States as some sort of Promised Land, so too, if the Young Left continues to insist on its pro-Arab Manicheism, the genuinely progressive and liberal-minded Jews in Western Europe and the United States will, in the long run, show a tendency to become affiliated with conservative movements who do not oppose Israel. I simplify slightly to drive home the point: should Georges Bidault one day really emerge as Israel's last friend, all those radical leftist French Jews who support the FLN[66] would, *la mort dans l'âme*,[67] from one day to the next cling to Bidault.[68] I could add some German examples but cannot overcome my reluctance to mention specific names in this context.

Nobody expects the Young Left to define itself in relation to "World Jewry." Nobody, least of all I, who always assumed I was closely aligned to it, demands that it take a pro-Jewish or pro-Israel position in the Israeli-Palestinian conflict, this historical tragedy without precedent. All I ask for is a minimum of goodwill and a basic sense of justice in its political judgments. Is it really that difficult to recognize that the generals of the Israeli Army are no Westmorelands?[69] Can one seriously liken the Israeli soldiers to the heroes of Lidice and Oradour?[70] Finally, is it really that much of an intellectual stretch to see that a game is being played out between the two superpowers in the Middle East in which Israelis and Arabs alike are mere pawns? Does it take a genius in sociology or political studies to understand that anti-Zionism gives antisemitism the inch that the whole mile will invariably have to follow? A pinch of common sense should suffice. One should not resign oneself to the notion that the Young Left has exchanged that pinch for unthinking dialectical phraseology and streamlined werewolf romanticism.

---

66 The Front de libération nationale (National Liberation Front) was the principal nationalist movement during the Algerian War.

67 Translation: with a heavy heart.

68 In 1961, Georges Bidault (1899–1983), who had in earlier years served as foreign and defense minister under de Gaulle, called for violent resistance against the Algerian national movement both in Algeria and in mainland France and denied the legitimacy of de Gaulle's government. He went underground and fled the country in 1962. He returned to France in 1968 after the authorities had suspended their arrest warrant against him.

69 General William Westmoreland (1914–2005) was the commander in charge of US military action in Vietnam from 1964 to 1968.

70 In 1942, following the assassination of Reinhard Heydrich, the Germans razed the Czech village of Lidice, murdering the inhabitants on the spot or sending them to the Chełmno extermination camp. In 1944, the Germans entirely destroyed the French village of Oradour-sur-Glane. Most of its inhabitants, including the women and children, were massacred by the Waffen-SS.

5 Jews, Leftists, Leftist Jews: The Changing Contours of a Political Problem (1973)

In a past whose end was marked brusquely by the year 1967, the matter seemed fairly simple: leftists and Jews—for all that many of the latter were conservative and, in a strict sociological sense, stood on the "right"—had an unspoken mutual understanding. Both were minorities, both belonged to the "damned of the earth." A certain mild antisemitic tradition on the left notwithstanding, notably in France (for in that country the name "Rothschild" is the cipher for capitalism), the socially and politically disenfranchised, on the one hand, and those excluded on religious and racial grounds, on the other, generally felt a sense of mutual solidarity. Not only were the left-wing (social democratic and communist) political parties frequently "managed" by Jews, a sizeable proportion of their grassroot supporters too tended to be Jewish. In his heart of hearts, even the most conservative Jew found it difficult to muster genuine resentment against the left since only left-wing groups and organizations rejected antisemitism on principle. Leftists were interested only in *man*, not in Germans, Frenchmen, or Englishmen etc. To the extent that the Jews felt recognized as human beings, they were confident that they could now be Germans, Frenchmen, or Englishmen too. Left-wing humanism with its disregard for ethnic, national, or religious distinctions promised not only universal human equality but also equality for the Jews within the nation state. The affinity between the left and the Jews, in turn, sprang not only from the fact that a significant number of left-wing theoreticians, from Marx, Bernstein, and Max Adler to Adorno and Marcuse, were of Jewish extraction but also from an instinctual sense that even among conservative Jews it had no fanatical foes.

* * *

This is now all in the deepest prehistorical past. Where do we stand today?

For the leftists, the situation seems to be pretty straightforward. Perhaps I can illustrate the current position with an episode I witnessed. I attended a discussion among the mostly leftist and far-left editors of the radio station of a small Western European country. It concerned Palestinian acts of terror. After several of the rather young members of the editorial team had condoned them with barely concealed enthusiasm, pointing to the legitimacy of the "counterviolence" deployed by the Palestinians, one young woman dared to raise a rather reticent objection. It was inappropriate, she suggested, simply to justify any and every kind of atrocity with the concept of counterviolence. Instead, one ought to determine on a case-by-case basis whether one could, in any given instance, speak in good faith of counterviolence or, conversely, counterviolence ran the risk of becoming violence per se and thus inhumane. An embarrassing and oppressive silence ensued until one of her interlocutors finally said, "I think you are incapable of understanding the conduct of the Palestinians. After all, your late husband was a Jew . . ." And thus the issue was turned into a matter of kinship liability. The young woman did not say another word, and I, being all the more *pars in causa*,[71] most certainly did not get involved.

Clearly, then, we have reached the point at which leftists no longer accept the word of a Jew—or, as one used to say, of a Jew's associate—when the problem of Israel is concerned because it automatically counts as prejudiced. Yet one might ask, What does the Jewish problem supposedly have to do with Israel? And are there no significant personalities on the New Left who, when it comes to the Middle East, are in complete agreement with the notions of their non-Jewish comrades? Do Ernest Mandel, Erich Fried, Alain Geismar, or Alain Krivine not exist?[72] Admittedly, though, they are, and of this I am fairly certain, no more characteristic of the general state of affairs than those Jews who collaborate with the Arab secret services or resistance organizations are of the domestic situation in Israel.

For the simple fact of the matter is that an existential bond (in the past one would have said a "bond of fate," which is actually not a bad epithet) connects the vast majority of Jews the world over to the state of Israel. It goes without saying that this bond has very little to do with unconditional support for everything the respective incumbent Israeli government does. I myself, for example, find the stubborn implacability with which Israel insists on its ownership of the Old City of Jerusalem bewildering; indeed, as a theological if not theocratic form of obsession, it makes me profoundly uncomfortable. I believe, and am hardly alone in doing so, that the various governments of the state of Israel have committed grave sins of omission by not developing a thought-out, humane, and progressive policy in relation to the Arabs when it was still possible. Neither do I agree with every repressive Israeli measure nor do I consider it a healthy state of affairs that the Israelis are turning themselves into a "master race" by importing Arab guest workers to support their economic and industrial expansion. To be sure, these workers are

---

71 Translation: party to the case.

72 The child of Polish Jewish immigrants, the Belgian Ernest Mandel (1923–1995) was a leading Trotskyite theoretician and played a prominent role in the Fourth International. Of Austrian Jewish parentage, the poet Erich Fried (1921–1988) fled Austria after the *Anschluss* and stayed in Britain for the rest of his life but played an active role in West Germany's cultural life. Alain Geismar (born 1939) is a physicist and activist who played a leading role in the protests in Paris in May 1968, as did the Trotskyite politician Alain Krivine (born 1941).

better off in material terms than they ever were back home and under their traditional leaders, but their circumstances are nevertheless disgraceful. These sorts of issues weigh on my leftist conscience, and I would like to see them resolved as soon as possible. And yet, I know that I have a deeply rooted interest in this country, even though I do not know it, do not speak its language, do not subscribe to its religion, and its folklore is as alien to me as that of some African tribe. This interest in Israel, which is shared by *all* Jews, is by no means irrational. Far from it: it can be readily accounted for in an entirely rational manner. The existence of the state of Israel has bestowed a new identity on every single Jew, even if he feels in no way shaped by his Jewishness. Since Israel exists, he knows that, contrary to the claims that the antisemite impressed on him for so long that he actually began to believe him, he is not cowardly, incapable of manual labor, suited only to the money trade, incapable of working the land, a driveling stay-at-home and, at best, a wisecracking chatterer. What is more, he knows that whenever and wherever his life might be in danger, there is a place on earth that would take him in, no matter what. He knows that as long as Israel exists, one will not be able to stick him into a fiery furnace again with the tacit support of the inhospitable host peoples or accompanied by their noncommittal pity, at best. He most certainly is "biased," then, where Israel is concerned. But does that render him completely deluded and necessarily unable to discuss the issue of Israel sensibly and with approximate objectivity? Is he invariably less discerning than his former friends on the left, those comrades who see nothing but the myth of the national resistance struggle and who show empathy for a deranged, book-burning Islamist fanatic of a dictator but not in the face of the mortal danger faced by every single Israeli?

A Jew, and all the more so a traditional *leftist* Jew, is, his connection to Israel notwithstanding, perfectly capable of discussing these issues with considerable reason and without succumbing to an undue emotional strain. The highly strung emotionalization of the issue, it seems to me, is, as things stand, largely a preserve of the New Left. For it, Israel is nothing but an outpost of American imperialism, and it operates as though General Dayan had personally ordered the razing of North Vietnamese towns, as though Israel were jointly responsible for every inhumane act committed by the American superpower in Latin America.

The truth is surely far removed from this Manichean notion. One might, if one so wishes, concede that the settlement of homeless Jews in Palestine was a grave historical injustice, a perfectly sinister and dastardly ruse of history. I have no opinion on this. All I know, as does anyone who has ever studied history, is that there are few states on this earth that do not owe their existence to some injustice. Today one can proceed only from the fact that the enormous efforts of endangered human beings have created Israel and that the destruction of this country, to which the Arab states aspire, whether they admit it or not, would create an inordinately more horrific injustice. As a Palestinian leader recently explained in an interview with *Le Monde*, "Israel is condemned to win every battle. If it loses just one, then . . ." He did not continue, but everyone knows that he was thinking of the angel of death who, in the event, would descend on the country. Israel, then, is fighting her own national liberation struggle against the Arab world, against a foe who is inordinately richer in terms of his population, money, and oil, and thus potentially more powerful. This struggle is at least as legitimate as that of the Palestinians. To the extent that the concept makes any sense, the force Israel exerts is itself a form of counterviolence. It is Israel's historical misfortune that she has only one ally in this liberation struggle: the United States. Israel did not have several options and chose this one. She simply grabbed the only hand that was stretched out in her direction and offering support. Can one seriously expect someone who is drowning to check whether there might be a bloodstain on the rescuing hand before seizing it?

All this is straightforward to the point of banality: one writes it down with the mild unease of somebody who is uncomfortable because all he can submit are self-evident truths. That it needs to be said all the same reflects no simple-mindedness on the part of the person saying it but, rather, the blindness to historical and humanitarian concerns displayed by a left that, in an unhealthy frenzy, has for years publicly denigrated and ultimately disavowed its noblest traditions. It seems to me that in the conflict between the left and the Jews, it is the responsibility of the *leftist Jews* who continue stubbornly to maintain their political identity to confront former comrades with a few elementary truths—truths that those former comrades will ultimately have to acknowledge, assuming they have not lost their grip on reality altogether. Let me summarize in a few sentences what I mean:

- Not every bomb thrown, not every hostage killed, is per se an act of superior political insight or a sign of heroism.
- Even when she sticks with the United States as the only ally on offer, Israel does not share the responsibility for all the political and military deeds and misdeeds of that ally.
- Not every Third World regime that calls itself revolutionary actually pursues genuine social-revolutionary policies. Algeria, which expelled the Black Panthers, is no more a revolutionary state than Gaddafi's Libya with its paroxysms of Islamic fanaticism.
- Anyone who questions Israel's right to exist is either too stupid to understand that he is contributing to or is intentionally promoting an über-Auschwitz.

6 The New Antisemitism (1976)

Is ANTISEMITISM BECOMING socially acceptable again? Only five years ago, this question would have seemed pretty absurd and, had Jews raised it, it would have been considered an expression of mild paranoia. It seems to me that this has changed dramatically since then. Antisemitism, rendered impossible to man and the world by something for which, in this discussion, I will use the shorthand "Auschwitz," is in the process of reinserting itself into political debates again and shamelessly gaining ground.

I do not mean the sort of antisemitism that has long been integral to the sociability of the German (and non-German) philistine who has always considered the "otherness" of the Jew, be it in the guise of a figure like Benjamin Disraeli or that of someone like Rathenau, repugnant, indeed, diabolical. In the eyes of both the little guy and his grand, influential counterpart, the Jewish people, branded as deicides—a bizarre notion that Christianity has disseminated with fanatical zeal on some occasions and in a dignified theological guise on others—always had been, and continued to be, an uncanny ethnic group, a religious community one could not trust. The antisemitism of the philistines has consistently been part of the magical worldview of peoples whom the Enlightenment passed by or who consciously suppressed it. It was not only the "socialism" of fools. It was also their metaphysics and social philosophy. The infamous *Protocols of the Elders of Zion* was only the most obvious and crude illustration of a collective mindset that, in the course of history, has become so deep-seated that even Marx could not escape it, and Otto Weininger, as the paradigmatic self-hating Jew, followed it through to its ultimate logical consequence and did away with himself.[73] This, then, is not the antisemitism that concerns me here. Or should it too need to be discussed after all? We will see. What is clear is that "classical" antisemitism was there first. Although it was implemented nowhere else in as bestial a manner as it was by the German Third Reich, it is a global phenomenon. In this context, I want to point in passing to Sartre's *Réflexions sur la question juive*,[74] to my mind still the last word on the analysis of this particular problem, which constitutes an even greater "stain on the honor" of civilized humanity than colonialism and imperialism.

---

73 Shortly after the publication of *Sex and Character*, in which he combined a plethora of antisemitic and misogynistic notions with an oddly perceptive critique of the projective nature of antisemitism and misogyny, the Viennese writer Otto Weininger (1880–1903) rented a room in the house in which Beethoven had died and there shot himself.

74 *Anti-Semite and Jew* (1946).

The antisemitism we are confronted with *today* does not speak its name. On the contrary: if one tries to hold it to account it disowns itself. It is no easy task to drag it before the court that has long since condemned it but would nevertheless need to be in constant session. How does the new antisemite present himself? His contention is extremely straightforward and, *prima facie*,[75] perfectly plausible: all claims to the contrary notwithstanding, he is no antisemite, he is in fact an *anti-Zionist!* With this, he assumes, he has salvaged his honor, all the more so because more than three decades have passed since Auschwitz gained its global notoriety. Consequently, the widespread moral outrage it precipitated has now lost its *élan vital*.[76] Even more importantly, the troubles in the Middle East have given rise to terrifyingly simplistic notions. Today's unabashedly bashful antisemite is in luck. The existence of the state of Israel, whose right to exist may be no more legitimate than that of any other state but neither is it *any less* well founded than that of its counterparts in the Christian and non-Christian world, provides him with convenient arguments. Have the Jews in Palestine not expelled a people, the Arab Palestinians, from its ancestral land? More importantly yet, are they not in the Palestinian territories, which they have acquired by military means, a brutal occupying power comparable to the Nazis who took control of most of Europe between 1940 and 1945? Are the Israelis not an outpost of global imperialism? Is their notion of statehood and nationhood not destined to lead to ever new wars of conquest? Is the struggle against Israel not part and parcel of the laudable progressive cause, as were the national liberation struggles of the Algerians or the Indonesian peoples? And is one not justified in being apprehensive about the Jews in general, given that, avowedly or not, they will ultimately always side with the tyrannical state of Israel? One can call out, "Strike the Zionist dead, make the Near East red!" and, while doing so, conceal, indeed, indignantly reject the insinuation that a further battle cry reverberates within this one: the Nazis' unambiguous "Perish Judah!"

It is never easy to argue a case when the other party, rather than a genuine willingness to enter into a debate, merely displays noxious bad faith. There would, to be sure, be plenty to discuss. Take, for example, the fact that there is not one—I choose my words carefully—*not a single state* on earth at whose inception legitimacy and illegitimacy, justice and injustice, did not become inextricably entwined. One might point to the fact that, in its role as an occupying power, Israel is surely quite humane, even when it comes to violent measures and possible acts of cruelty that may have been committed. As a fundamental historical evil, such incidents stain the record of every state that has ever had to administer hostile territory. Anyone who does not understand this should be forced to study the history of the German occupation in Holland, Norway, France, Denmark, and so on or the French occupation of the Ruhr between 1923 and 1925. Yet would this compulsory study

---

75 Translation: on the face of it.
76 Translation: life force.

of history make the spurious slogans, the misguided analogies, and the ridiculous prejudices disappear? I rather doubt it. I doubt it, and this brings me back to my main line of argument, because anti-Zionism is nothing other than an updated version of the age-old and evidently ineradicable, utterly irrational hatred that has been directed against the Jews since time immemorial. In his remarkable book *Outsiders*,[77] the German philologist and social philosopher Hans Mayer wrote that "whoever attacks Zionism, but by no means wishes to say anything against the Jews, is fooling himself or others." One should add that the "fooling oneself" of the anti-Zionists, who are invariably antisemites too, draws on historical or, one might say, collective psychological presuppositions that are not amenable to reasoned debate. The antisemite both wants to see radical evil in the Jew and is compelled by these presuppositions to do so. In this context, a usurer serving a princely ruler is no less suitable as an object of hatred than an Israeli general. For the antisemite, the Jew must always be gotten rid of, no matter what he actually does. Compelled to be a merchant, he is considered a bloodsucker. If he is an intellectual, he supposedly subverts the existing world order with diabolical intent. As a soldier, he is a colonialist, as a soldier, a cruel oppressor. If he is willing to assimilate into his respective host society, the antisemite considers him a dishonorable interloper. If the Jew too lays claim to that fashionable and much celebrated phenomenon, a "national identity," one calls him a racist.

These are, alas, issues that have been well known for decades. Smart people from Masaryk to Sartre have analyzed them with ample clarity. New, at best, is the shameful fact that the antisemitism claiming to be mere anti-Zionism has its most unrestrained proponents in the political camp one would least suspect of antisemitic sentiments: on the political *left*. Not that the political right has ceased to be antisemitic. It falls under the category I previously referred to as the "philistines." As ever, those on the right are willing to offer the Jews cautious toleration, at best, and likely to engage in crude antisemitic violence, at worst. However, with the exception of the card-carrying old Nazis, they do not (yet) dare step forward with sufficient forthrightness to allow their stance to be pinned down. They seem to be pussyfooting around yesterday's hot but currently no more than lukewarm topic, confident that their hour will eventually come.

Will their hour come? Has it possibly arrived already? Such questions can be answered only with the greatest caution. Prophecies are obviously off-limits, but it is certainly legitimate to express one's concerns. Let us begin with the unquestionable fact that leftists are now the most eloquent proponents of anti-Zionism in all its brutishness. This begins with the German Social Democrats' youth organization, which is vigorously pushing the older comrades in the party to issue

---

77 Hans Mayer, *Outsiders: A Study in Life and Letters* (Cambridge, MA: MIT Press, 1984), 394 (translation amended).

anti-Zionist statements and extends all the way to the orthodox Soviet Communists, Maoists, Trotskyites, and various sectarian groups of independent radical leftists. How the Soviets treat their Jewish citizens is well known the world over. Like the Nazis before them, they imagine that each and every Jew is embroiled in a Zionist-imperialist world conspiracy. The New Left operating outside of the Soviet sphere of influence, insofar as it is genuinely independent of the Soviets (of which I am not entirely convinced), shares the Soviet perception, though it does articulate it in a terminologically more refined manner, which is, however, no less radical for it. One should bear in mind that European terrorists are frequently trained in the use of Soviet weapons in Palestinian settlements euphemistically called "refugee camps" and that anti-Zionist kidnappers regularly find refuge in Soviet-aligned Arab countries when their work is done.[78] They are united in refusing, time and again, to profess their antisemitism, and I am perfectly willing to concede that they are not consciously motivated by antisemitic resentment or, to be more precise, that they do not recognize their antisemitic sentiments as such. Yet their conviction that they are anti-Zionists, motivated by the injustices perpetrated, to their mind, on the Palestinians and not, in any conventional sense, antisemites evidently does not run all that deep. For even a modicum of intellectual probity would suffice to let them appreciate that each and every Jew feels a kind of existential bond with the state of Israel and its sovereign existence, regardless of whether he belongs to the Mosaic religious community or not, regardless of whether he supports or rejects Zionism.

There are two reasons for this, neither of which has anything to do with metaphysics, a neurotic sense of election, or racism. The state of Israel is a commonwealth that has taught the Jews not to allow their self-perception to be impressed on them by the antisemites. It is the country where the Jew is not a usurer but a farmer, not a pale stay-at-home but a soldier, not a wholesale merchant but a craftsman. Thanks to the state of Israel, the Jews in the Soviet Union and the United States, in France and wherever else the winds of the diaspora may have taken them, have grasped that they are human beings like all others. No more and no less. The second, no less clearly defined reason for the Jews' attachment to the tiny state in the Middle East is this: for two millennia they were endangered and dependent on the non-Jews' gaze. Occasionally they benefited from the non-Jews' good faith. More often, they were at the receiving end of their pronounced ill will. Like dark thunderclouds, the threat of expulsion, of a humiliating death, which they stood no chance of resisting, loomed over them. And in the Third Reich, one of those thunderclouds eventually wreaked the most gruesome catastrophe on the Jews. Since the state of Israel exists, the Jews have a virtual asylum to fall back on,

---

78 In the early 1970s, members of the German Red Army Faction went to Jordan, where they trained with guerrilla fighters from the Popular Front for the Liberation of Palestine and Palestine Liberation Organization.

no matter what. I emphasize the term *virtual*. After all, history does not simply repeat itself like a film on an endless loop, and the rise of another Hitler is unlikely in the extreme. Jews in the United States, for instance, to the intense frustration of radical Zionists and the Israeli government, show no serious intention of swapping the land of milk and honey for the arid, dusty, and stony land of Israel. France's Jews are French Jews in the way Germany's Jews were once German Jews. If only they were granted the full rights of Soviet citizens, even the Soviet Jews wanting to emigrate to the entirely alien state of Israel would be few and far between.

What is important to all of them is the *option*, the existence of a potential asylum. Anyone who has ever lost his home and roamed the earth in search of refuge will understand this. Is it unreasonable to expect that young leftists, who are generally well versed in sociology and psychology, should be particularly well placed to empathize with the situation of a group of human beings who have been humiliated for two millennia? Given that most of them have benefited from higher education and acquired some knowledge of history, should not they of all people be able to comprehend that the Palestinian question merely requires a technical solution? The Jewish state, by contrast, buffeted as it is by so much hatred, would, should it founder, bequeath to its inhabitants nothing but the slaughtering knife of their opponents, opponents whose socialization has already prepared them for the murder of the Jews. I am convinced, though I cannot prove it, that the leftist anti-Zionists/antisemites actually have a clear sense of all this, but they repress it. This process of repression, culminating in their indifference toward the catastrophic fate of the Jews, actually brings us right back to the time-worn antisemitism of the philistines, which amounts to little more than a form of oafishness when things are running smoothly but paves the way for the sorts of bestialities we have witnessed when the going gets tough. It is positively tragic that on this issue the left is doing the bidding of its opponents, in part because of its mindlessness and ideological stubbornness, and in part, I would argue, as a result of a widespread and enduring European antisemitic tradition. Given the historical and moral pathos with which it presents itself, the new form of anti-semitism is much more dangerous than the old antisemitism, the antisemitism of the philistines, which it is so eager to serve. We are indeed dealing with a *dialectic* at this point. It is high time that the professional dialecticians recognize this and recover their ability to position themselves in a manner worthy of their humanity.

7 Shylock, Kitsch, and Its Hazards (1976)

SILLINESS IS BY no means invariably harmless. Trash that dare not speak its name becomes kitsch, in other words: art, which is none. We are dealing here with Genet *sans génie*,[79] a pseudo-Paris that has descended on Frankfurt, undigested Georges Bataille, transgression at bargain basement prices, and an ingenuous injection of the Berlin of the Threepenny Opera.[80] To make things worse, the whole thing is recited, quite ridiculously, as though it were a play by Büchner. Keep it, with your other treasures.[81] Were it not for its outright antihero, *the rich Jew*, this play by Fassbinder would merit no attention at all.[82]

Is this an antisemitic play? Hardly. It goes without saying that Fassbinder was no more intent on writing something antisemitic than the rather more serious novelist Zwerenz, by whose book about the moonlike uninhabitability of Frankfurt he was inspired.[83] Fassbinder's rich Jew is presented in a less tendentious manner than Shakespeare's *Merchant of Venice*, Marlowe's *Jew of Malta*, or Hauff's *Jud Süß*. In fact, were it not for the aforementioned silliness of the entire enterprise, this loaded crook from Frankfurt would basically emerge as the tragic figure in the play, and the tragic, as is well known, transcends moral categories. It is obvious that Fassbinder is no antisemite. But as the author of this play, he is a bad dramatist; he is, and this, for the purposes of our discussion, is the crux of the matter, void of psychological and philosophical insight

---

79 Lit. *uninspired*. In French the noun *sans-génie* means "sap," "fool," or "simpleton." This may be a reference to a poem in Nietzsche's *Beyond Good Evil* (1886, section 228). In Walter Kaufmann's translation it reads, "Hail, dear drudge and patient fretter!/'More drawn out is always better,'/Stiffness grows in head and knee/No enthusiast and no joker/Indestructibly mediocre,/*Sans genie et sans esprit!*"

80 A reference to Bertold Brecht's play *The Threepenny Opera* (1928).

81 This is a line from Schiller's drama *Love and Intrigue* (*Kabale und Liebe*, 1784). In act 2, scene 2, a valet brings one of the female protagonists a gift from the ruler, who has paid for the valuable jewels by pressing men (including the valet's two sons) into military service abroad. Assuming that she intends to keep the gift, her demonstrative indignation notwithstanding, the valet refuses the reward she offers him for his services with these words, throwing the money back on the table "with contempt."

82 Rainer Werner Fassbinder, "Der Müll, die Stadt und der Tod" [Garbage, the city and death] in *Stücke* 3 (Frankfurt/Main: Suhrkamp, 1976).

83 Gerhard Zwerenz, *Die Erde ist unbewohnbar wie der Mond* [Earth is as uninhabitable as the moon] (Frankfurt/Main: Fischer, 1973).

and proceeds in an ahistorical manner. What the play lazily rehearses and is embodied in the figure of the rich Jew has nothing to do with Frankfurt. To be sure, as I have just been told, there are criminals of Jewish descent in Frankfurt. There are also Jewish criminals in Tel Aviv, where the authorities ruthlessly prosecute crooks of this kind who deal in properties and prostitutes. Yet what does that mean: Jewish crooks? Not a lot. I can easily imagine a form of journalistic or literary outrage directed at those who act to the detriment of the city in which the word *Jew* does not feature, not because some taboo prohibits it but for the simple reason that the Jewish extraction of these criminals has nothing, absolutely nothing, to do with the havoc they wreak. Indeed, insofar as it was ever anything other than an *empty* myth, a skeletal specter, the "rich Jew" has long since ceased to function as an empirically grounded foil for the projection of fictional fabrications. If the play had been truly realistic and named the crook who remains anonymous in the play, showing no fear of the libel trial that would likely have ensued, then and only then would it have been legitimate to refer to the "Jew X," albeit with psychological mastery and a sense of historical responsibility.

Is all this a matter of "left-wing fascism"? I recommend caution. I am not going to start arguing vociferously that "snow is black" just because Joachim Fest suggests that snow is white.[84] I cannot see any "left-wing fascism" in Fassbinder's play. I do fear, however, that such uncouth nullities will give a boost to the widespread *latent* antisemitism often masquerading as anti-Zionism, which is by no means a preserve of the Germans. Even an unsuccessful Shylockian play can promote antisemitic tendencies, beginning with those of the philistine's coven and leading all the way to the graduate seminar and the commune. An intelligent author would have appreciated this. Fassbinder is young. This is no more his fault than I can claim credit for my advanced age. One cannot hold it against him that he did not experience National Socialism. But he could easily have obtained the relevant documents that would have allowed him to recognize that one should not play with a fire that exudes toxic gas.

The author we meet in *Garbage, the City and Death* is no persecutor of Jews. Those familiar with the German scene, and I suppose I have to take their word for it, assure me that he is no leftist either. But he is clueless, and the sort of "anticapitalism" presented in this play is so simplistic that it could drive even Sartre into the arms of Raymond Aron. That Fassbinder did not opt for the "rich citizen of Düsseldorf," compared to whom the "rich Jew" is a destitute wretch, and chose instead to pull the timeworn figure of Shylock out of the fusty closet is about as

---

84 Following the publication of his acclaimed Hitler biography in 1973, the historian and journalist Joachim Fest (1926–2006) became one of the editors of the West German center-right quality daily *Frankfurter Allgemeine Zeitung*, where he published his harsh critique of Fassbinder's play on March 19, 1976.

far removed from socialism, as "right wing," as one can be. However, what does bear noting and emphasizing is this: the Marxist dilettantes who doggedly present themselves as "leftists," the *homines ludentes* of revolution,[85] are not without responsibility for this tomfoolery. After all, they are the sounding board the author is playing to, presumably without realizing that he has in fact written his Shylockian show for the German house, a house whose brown walls have been given a perfunctory lick of new paint at best. Whatever Fest or the left may think, this is a dangerous play. The losers in this game are those who identify with an authentic left and have to look on as the philistines' coven, which is ultimately as opposed to the left as it is antisemitic, capitalizes on the play at the same time as the powers that be, with the serene conscience of the antisemite of yesteryear and today, make a killing trading with the Arabs.

Both Fassbinder and Fest mock the eternal losers of the old, genuine left who are not faring well as they continue to knock on the doors of deaf men. They have no interest in seeing this play withdrawn. Far from it. They were keen to observe whether the Germans would react as they expect. For all they still can do, as and until they make their exit, is observe and continue to observe.

---

85 Translation: playing men or men who play. This is a reference to the cultural theorist Johan Huizinga (1872–1945), who stressed the integral cultural and social significance of playing and playfulness.

8 Virtuous Antisemitism: Address on the Occasion of Jewish-Christian Brotherhood Week (1976)

I COME TO you to speak about the Jewish Question at a point in time when it has apparently resurfaced on a global scale, so these are hardly times that bode well for the thoughts I want to share with you. This is, then, *Jewish-Christian Brotherhood Week*.[86] Yet where are the brothers? If I were more of a cynic, I might quote the American mathematician and chansonnier Tom Lehrer, who, some years ago, on the occasion of an American "Brotherhood Week," sang, "And the Catholics hate the Protestants and the Protestants hate the Catholics and the Muslims hate the Hindus—and everybody hates the Jews." Fortunately, we have not yet reached the point at which the Jews, as an ethnic group and religious community, are subject to a generalized form of burning hatred. Even so, that point is *not as far off* as the optimists assume. What is already demonstrable is a general feeling of unease vis-à-vis the Jews. The misgivings even, perhaps especially, of people who only ten years ago were presenting themselves in a rather tedious manner as philosemites have become palpable in disquieting ways. Antisemitism can draw on a historically and psychologically deeply rooted collective infrastructure. If it is currently re-inventing itself, three decades after the discovery of the Nazis' actions, this is due not only to the amount of time that has passed since and is silently and inces-santly eroding the ethical outrage but also, and perhaps principally, to the devel-opments in the *Middle East*. Particularly appalling is the fact that it is the *young people*, and notably those among them who consider themselves socialists in the broadest sense of the word, who are testing our credulity by resorting to this ancient hatred long since considered obsolete. Take the current debate within the Second International, which has traditionally been well-disposed toward the Jews and supported Israel. The young socialists, for whom the Palestinians are today the freedom fighters and the Israelis the imperialist oppressors, are de-manding that the Second International distance itself from Israel. For the Third International, this goes without saying anyway. It considers Israel a cancerous imperialist growth and the Jews more generally permanent accomplices of the

---

86 The Woche der Brüderlichkeit (Brotherhood Week or, lit., Week of Brotherliness) is an event promoting Christian-Jewish understanding in (initially West) Germany that has been taking place annually since 1952.

capitalist conspiracy. Its leader, the Soviet Union, issued the orders, and the Third International followed suit.

One might well object that Israel has nothing to do with the Jewish problem in general. All this is not an issue of *antisemitism but of anti-Israelism*. This objection is easily, indeed, all too easily dismissed. Let me quote the German philologist Hans Mayer, a man steeped in the knowledge of Marxism.[87] In his remarkable book *Outsiders*, he writes,

> Whoever attacks Zionism, but by no means wishes to say anything against the Jews, is fooling himself or others. The state of Israel is a Jewish state. Whoever wants to destroy it, avowedly or by means of a policy, which cannot but result in its annihilation, is dealing in the anti-Jewish hatred that has been with us since time immemorial. The extent to which this is reflected in the interplay of domestic and foreign policy is demonstrated by the domestic policies of the current anti-Zionist states. It is predicated on the assumption that their own Jewish citizens are virtual Zionists and harasses them accordingly.[88]

I was recently struck, while reading the French daily *Le Monde*, as I do every day, by the extent to which anti-Zionism taps into the traditional antisemitic and anti-Jewish hallucinations. In this particular issue, the paper's special correspondent for the Middle East, Michel Tatu, quoted from a photo spread published by the Egyptian government to mark the second anniversary of the Yom Kippur War. The passage in question explained that "the world over, one does not want Jews to enter the military . . . because they always prioritize money over principles. . . . Usurers are no warriors." One should resist the temptation to laugh about the fact that this is the voice of a country that was rescued only by the massive pressure exerted on Israel by the United States when push came to shove in October 1973. More importantly, however, as Tatu pointed out, these remarks were, relatively speaking, moderate in character. In the "tougher" Arab states, in Syria, Iraq, or Algeria, the prevalent rhetoric was inordinately more aggressive. It goes without saying that all this no longer bears the slightest semblance to "normal" territorial disputes between sovereign states such as the conflict between Algeria and Morocco, say. It is pure Streicher, antisemitism both of the most reprehensible and the most idiotic kind. Yet we must bear in mind, alas, that causes that were both reprehensible and idiotic have triumphed more than once in world history and that one can place no trust whatsoever in the assurances to the contrary of one Professor Georg Wilhelm Friedrich Hegel.

87 Hans Mayer (1907–2001) was one of the most important Marxist literary scholars of the twentieth century. While both his parents were murdered in Auschwitz, he survived the Nazi period in exile in France and Switzerland. Following his return to Germany, he held a chair in literary studies in Leipzig (East Germany) before defecting to West Germany in 1963, where he taught at the Polytechnic in Hannover.
88 Hans Mayer, *Outsiders: A Study in Life and Letters* (Cambridge, MA: MIT Press, 1982), 394 (translation amended).

Provided it dresses itself up as anti-Zionism, young people are happy to align themselves with this reprehensible and idiotic antisemitism. We are not dealing here with a handful of youngsters led astray by their unreconstructed Nazi parents and grandparents but with ostensible socialists. And nobody is opposing them in a sufficiently energetic manner. Far from it. The bourgeoisie, whether in Germany, in France, or in Belgium, is breathing a sigh of relief that for once it can march in step with a young generation it generally considers a nuisance, given its anti-authoritarian predilections. Aside from its own deeply rooted latent antisemitism, the bourgeoisie is pursuing its own vested interests, which coincide in a seamless and gratifying manner with the thoughtless antisemitism of the youngsters, most of whom have never met a Jew in person. It is interested in trade, mainly in oil. It is high time to "come down on the right side," as these people would say. The multinational corporations who in all the Western democracies, in contravention of the law but fully in keeping with commercial principles, are more than happy to comply with the Arab boycott demands, know full well that *les affairs sont les affairs*.[89] Assuming they have heard of the concept, they too are pleased to be moving with the objective spirit for once. Thus, antisemitism is becoming what, since the exposure of the Nazi atrocities, it no longer was or could be: a *virtue*.

To be sure, antisemitism *qua* antisemitism might well have found it more difficult to regain its current level of respectability were it not for the deep-seated and, if I may use this much-abused term, *existential* bond between the Jews, every single one of them, and the state of Israel. I must instantly qualify my contention that this concerns "every single one of them." Wherever you look, you will, of course, find a handful of dutifully self-hating Jews who, in the service of some ideological fantasy or equally illusory and suicidal "objectivity," are prepared to dispute this sense of solidarity, even while it applies to them too. These special cases apart, and they tend to call for pity rather than condemnation, a bond ties the Jews, regardless of whether they are religious or not, whether they support or reject Zionism, whether they arrived in their host countries only recently or settled there long ago, to Israel's fortunes and misfortunes. I myself am a fairly typical case. I have never belonged to any Jewish religious community and was brought up a Catholic. I have no relatives in Israel, and my pending visit there will be my first. I come from a family that had long since established itself in Vorarlberg. Germany was once my cultural home; France has since replaced it. I have lived in Belgium for thirty-eight years. And yet: if there is one state and commonwealth on earth whose existence and independence genuinely concerns me, it is Israel. Needless to say, this results not from bizarre mythical notions regarding blood ties and racial belonging. The crucial point is this: the existence of a Jewish state whose inhabitants are not just merchants but also farmers, not just intellectuals but also professional soldiers,

---

89 Translation: business is business.

who are not the "usurers" the new Egypt is blathering about, all the empirical evidence to the contrary notwithstanding, but, for the most part, craftsmen and industrial or agricultural proletarians, has taught the Jews the world over to hold their heads high. The USSR and its vassal states have done everything within their power to cure the Jews of Marxism-Leninism. One need only think of the fate of Leopold Trepper, the erstwhile head of the intelligence organization Rote Kapelle, a convinced Marxist through and through, who eventually, when he was driven out of his Polish homeland, sought and found refuge in Israel.

Which brings me to the issue of refuge. For there is indeed more at stake than the Jews' upright gait. Israel is not only the country in which the Jew no longer has his self-image impressed on him by his enemy in the manner described by Sartre. It is also the virtual refuge for all the humiliated and libeled Jews the world over. A case in point are the Jews in the Soviet Union and the countries of the Warsaw Pact for whom, given their despair, an exit visa for Israel embodies their last remaining hope that they might yet lead their lives in dignity and an at-mosphere of civility. I emphasize that this hope is *virtual*. If their rights as Soviet citizens were no longer curtailed, only a small percentage of Soviet Jews would presumably want to settle in Israel, just as only very few American Jews are keen to move to the Mediterranean country Thomas Mann described as "dusty and stony." *Yet the existence of this virtual refuge is of crucial importance.* The option of finding refuge in Israel, should some sinister fiend determined to expel the Jews emerge somewhere, an option the authorities during the British mandate denied many of the Jews fleeing Hitler, this option connects each and every Jew to the fate of this tiny state in the Middle East. What, I wonder, would Messrs. Maxime Rodinson, Ernest Mandel, or Eric Rouleau, all of them ideologically alienated anti-Israeli Jews, do should they be threatened by a new Hitler?[90] They would turn up in an Israeli consulate, groveling pitifully for the documents that would allow them to rescue their skin and no longer give a damn about Marx's antisemitic misguided comments, which currently still form part of their canon. This is all I will say on what I have called the *existential bond* that ties all Jews to the state of Israel, a bond that has nothing whatsoever to do with some national-ist or religious form of mysticism, which would indeed be entirely illusory. My discussion is predicated on very real political, social, and psychological facts.

I can already hear the objections. "*What about the Arabs?* What about their state? What about their national dignity?" I hear you ask, and these are legiti-

---

90 The son of Eastern European Jewish immigrants, both of whom were murdered in Auschwitz, Maxime Rodinson (1915–2004) was a Marxist intellectual and held a chair in Old Ethiopic and South Arabian languages at the Sorbonne. The Cairo-born journalist Eric Rouleau worked for the Middle East service of Agence France Presse from 1953 to 1960 and from 1956 onward as a reporter (and later columnist) for *Le Monde*. His influence on the reporting of the Israeli-Pal-estinian conflict in France was considerable. Under President Mitterrand, he served as France's ambassador to Tunisia and Turkey. Both Rodinson and Rouleau were staunch anti-Zionists.

mate concerns that need to be addressed. I am no Middle East expert and know no more about the history of Zionism than the next man who reads the papers. My limited knowledge is quite sufficient, however, to let me draw a number of conclusions that those who depend on their common sense and experts in the field alike will find equally plausible, provided their perspective has not been distorted by ideological concerns. The Palestinians, who did not exist as a national group when the first Zionist immigrants arrived in what is today Israel, are now undertaking the process of nation building, and they are *entitled* to their own state. The Arabs living within Israel's borders as they were prior to the Six-Day War are *owed the right* not to be treated as second-class citizens. As I have previously stated elsewhere, in this conflict, *legitimate claim is pitted against legitimate claim*. Even so, one should not lose sight of the fact that it would, *in principle*, present no insurmountable difficulties to meet the claims of the Palestinians, those who live within Israel's original pre-1948 borders and those who were displaced from their homes by the wars for which their Arab brethren are surely in no small measure responsible. What would it take? We need the former to be loyal Israeli citizens. And we need the latter finally and unreservedly to accept the existence of the Jewish nation state. All other issues are of a purely technical nature and could therefore be resolved with a reasonable measure of intelligence and goodwill. And what, finally, would we need from the public that, across the spectrum from the extreme right to the extreme left, so readily condemns Israel in the name of the right to national self-determination and national identity? It need merely acknowledge the self-evident fact that the much-maligned Zionist movement too is a national liberation movement and that the Jews, who are the most tormented and tragic people on earth, are entitled to their national identity too, assuming, that is, that they are searching for it. Alternatively, they may, in both religious and ethnic terms, have merged fully into their host societies. This too is a perfectly respectable solution, although it obviously takes two to play: the willingness to merge must be met by a willingness to absorb those intent on merging.

The alarming banality of all this makes it no less true. Contrary to Adorno's warped contention that the banal can never be true,[91] it is in fact *always true*. How else would the banal have become commonplace? I repeat: in the conflict in the Middle East, *legitimate claim is pitted against legitimate claim*. I would add, however, that *the two parties are not endangered in equal measure*. Be it in the guise of the Saudi despot who is circulating the *Protocols of the Elders of Zion*, the religiously obsessed Gaddafi, the ostensibly "moderate" Sadat, or the self-avowed Marxist Habash, the fact of the matter is that the Arab nation is hell-bent on eradicating the state of Israel, rather like one Herr Göring once hoped to do

---

91 This is a reference to Theodor W. Adorno's essay, "Meinung Wahn Gesellschaft" (1961).

with the English cities.[92] It is an equally incontrovertible truth that there is no one on this planet who would raise the alarm if a new genocide were imminent. No one at all? This is obviously not entirely true. There are, for instance, public figures such as Jean-Paul Sartre and Simone de Beauvoir, widely recognized as lackeys of imperialism, who have taken issue with the shameless decisions of the UN and UNESCO.[93] And there are a handful of others like them. But they have no power. Where power resides, from the White House in Washington to the Palais d'Elysée, from Downing Street to the Kremlin, where one has long since forgotten that the majority of those who forged the old Russia into the fatherland of all proletarians were Jews, one is, not to put too fine a point on the diplomatic language, happy to defend the "rights of the Arabs," which can be measured in Petrodollars, while selling the rights of the Jews, which have, after all, been the eternal bane of the poor, for a few silver coins.

This kind of realpolitik—in France one uses the term *la Realpolitik* to denote despicable opportunism—is inexorably seeping into the circulatory system of what we call public opinion, which, as we know from sociological research, consists only of opinions about opinions. The recent behavior of the Christian denominations and the Vatican in particular is a case in point for this shift in public opinion, which not so long ago was well-disposed toward the Jews and Israel. The "deputy"[94] misses no opportunity to express his sympathies for the Palestinians, yet, to the best of my knowledge, he never protested when the corpses of Christians were mutilated in the context of the Lebanese civil war and remained silent when Palestinian commandos murdered Jewish youngsters.

In February 1976, at an Islamic-Christian gathering that took place in Gaddafi's Tripoli of all places, representatives of the Vatican, despite some initial trepidation, subserviently signed up to a generalized condemnation of Israel, which could just as well have been formulated by Gaddafi himself. It denounced Zionism yet again as a form of racism and included the following statement regarding Jerusalem: "The Islamic character of Jerusalem has been firmly established. . . . The Judaization, partition and internationalization of the Holy City must all be avoided." It was like a bad dream, as though the nightmare of a united Muslim and Christian Crusade against Israel and the Jews had come true. To be sure, the Vatican subsequently renounced the document its representatives had inexplicably

---

92 In 1970, Anwar Sadat (1918–1981) succeeded Nasser as Egypt's president. In 1978, he and Menachem Begin received the Nobel Peace Prize in recognition of their work toward the Israeli-Egyptian peace treaty finally signed the following year. Sadat was assassinated by Islamists in October 1981. George Habash (1926–2008) was the founder of the People's Front for the Liberation of Palestine.

93 Simone de Beauvoir strongly opposed the decision of UNESCO's General Assembly in 1974 to exclude Israel from a regional working group because it had undertaken archeological excavations.

94 This is a reference to Rolf Hochhuth's drama *The Deputy* (1964), in which he took issue with the Vatican's failure to act in the face of the Shoah.

signed. It even went one step further: at a gathering of Catholic and Jewish theologians in Jerusalem, Rome adopted a position that came close to being supportive of Israel. Even so, this hardly erases the parley in Tripoli from collective memory. Nor does the Vatican's recantation detract from what one of the Muslim interlocutors in Tripoli told Western journalists in a private conversation: "The Vatican is isolated," he said, "and desperately depends on the goodwill of the densely populated and extremely powerful Muslim world."

It is indeed the fascination with power that has brought about the change of heart. Given that everyone knows how arduous it is to do so, no one wants to row against the flow. Hence, those who are willing still to profess what seemed self-evident only yesterday but is considered outlandish today are few and far between. Only a moment ago, it seemed natural to support the Israelis' right to their own state. Suddenly one is struck by the fact that this support has become a veritable test of courage. Indeed, tomorrow it might well be considered positively offensive. Whether it is the man who holds political responsibility, the cautious journalist, or the politically interested interlocutor on the street, they all look into the round in anticipation, as though to ask, With what, and how much of it, can I already get away again? To those for whom this process cannot go quickly enough, anyone who is familiar with the issue and has some intuition for the vacillations of the constantly vacillating will be inclined to offer the reassurance that there is already a great deal with which they can not only get away but which is positively expected of them. Others, too clever by half, express their relief at the fact that a taboo has been broken, oblivious to the sinister forces whose bidding they are doing.

The problem, and with this I return to my main line of argument, is that all this, the self-alienation of the left, the interests of international big business and the powers that be, the malice of the rulers and the rapturous elation of the ruled and disinherited, it all resonates with a world in which, as it ever was, the Jew is burned.[95] It resonates with the expression of what the Nazis would have called the "sound will of the people" in Harlem (New York), with the gatherings of philistines in the Fürths of the world, with the Café de Commerce in Dijon, with some random godforsaken dump in Kent, and all the more so with any given Arab bazaar.

At this juncture, please allow me to digress. The supporters of the Arab cause frequently argue that in the world of Islam, in contrast to the Christian occident, the Jews have always coexisted peacefully and amicably with the Muslims. Albert Memmi, a Tunisian Jew who lives in France and has persistently championed the cause of the North African Arabs under French rule, has demonstrated quite incontrovertibly in a richly documented book that this was by no means the case.[96]

---

95 See footnote 47.
96 Albert Memmi, *Juifs et Arabes* (Paris: Gallimard, 1974).

Under Muslim rule, the Jews were always second-class citizens. Where they were able to work their way up the ranks, as was the case in Al-Andalus,[97] their status nevertheless continued to be precarious. At best, they were tolerated, but they were never genuinely accepted. This has not changed. It is possible for a communist who is also an Arab nationalist to be elected as mayor of an Israeli town. Yet in Syria or Iraq or even in Tunisia, which is supposedly more moderate, all of them countries where the remaining Jews are no less indigenous than their Arab oppressors, the few Jews who still live there are subject to habitual humiliation, and their existence is under constant threat. The Christian world is no more interested in them than it is in the Soviet Jews. In both cases, the path of total assimilation is no more an option than is flight to the country that they still consider, even under extremely difficult economic circumstances, the "promised land."

Being the existentialist, the positivist, and the adamantine atheist I am, I would not dream of treating the Jews' lot as some sort of metaphysical issue. As far as I am concerned, the Jews are no more chosen than they are cursed. They are no more than the contingent product of two millennia worth of unfavorable historical constellations. The history of the human species is so vast it eludes comprehensive reconstruction. By these standards, two millennia constitute an extraordinarily brief time span. I can just see a man like Lévi-Strauss, who studies prehistoric societies and their structural myths, smiling placidly and with mild disdain at such, from his perspective, micro-temporal processes.[98] Presumably, this particular member of the Académie Française would be disabused of this smile only if somebody were forcefully to bang on his door and issue the curt order that he, the Jew, must immediately open up and come along. Should he assume this could not happen to him, he would be quite mistaken. As is well known, Henri Bergson too, a man of even greater stature, was forced to wear the yellow star until death was kind enough to spare him the worst. No, the Jews and their historical existence are not metaphysical issues. As I say, they are the victims of contingency rather than necessity and of the same "inertia of the heart" that has bestowed unspeakable misery on the medieval peasant and the proletarian in the developed capitalist order. I am consciously enlisting the antiquated term *inertia of the heart* because it does a better job of summarizing the relevant issues than do even the most ingenious socio-psychological studies on the matter. Those of you who are slightly older may recall witnessing how, during the Third Reich, laziness of the heart allowed people quickly to get used to the fact that their Jewish neighbors were being taken away in the dark of night and deported. Today,

---

97 The Arabic name for the medieval Iberian peninsula under Muslim rule.

98 Claude Lévi-Strauss (1908–2009) was a prominent social anthropologist and leading structuralist. In 1941, he was able to flee France (on the same boat as André Breton, Anna Seghers, and Victor Serge) to Martinique and from there to New York, where he taught at the New School before returning to France after the war.

anyone can observe how the inert hearts are accommodating themselves to the fact that the capitalist and socialist worlds alike are *isolating* the Israelis and the Jews affiliated with them, *no matter where they are,* and, in so doing, abandoning them to the catastrophe looming over them like a thundercloud. The Middle Eastern Question has suddenly become a new Jewish Question, and we know from history what the answer to this question looks like. The cautious but unambiguous manner in which everyone is backing away both from Israel and, with it, from all Jews will hardly surprise someone who has encountered inert hearts before. The millions of Jews presented as burnt offerings—and what if there really were "only" five or even four, and not six, million of them?—have been paid off. Surely these perpetual gadflies should now keep their peace. We have other problems: recession, inflation, unemployment, energy problems. One left the wretch to fall: woe will befall him,[99] and the world, in the manner of Pontius Pilate, will wash its hands of him. Antisemitism in the guise of anti-Zionism has come to be seen as virtuous. This is not the place to discuss its roots. Everyone is familiar with them; they have received ample attention. I just want to emphasize what I have observed in many radio and television programs and newspaper articles. With an inert heart, one pretends not to know of the *existential connection* between diaspora Jewry and Israel. One obtusely refuses to recognize that this union of desperation is not some fantastical folly but simply reflects the fact that the once-bitten Jew knows in his heart of hearts where to find the closest and only emergency room willing to treat him.

The virtuous antisemite has an enviably clear conscience and a perfectly calm disposition. His peace of mind is enhanced further by the fact that he knows he is in step with the historical development. Should he occasionally awaken from his stupor, he ritualistically raises the usual questions. Is Israel not an expansionist state, an imperialist outpost? Has it not caused the adversity it faces from all sides itself, given the "inflexibility" of its policies? Did not the original sin of colonialism inhere in the Zionist idea from the outset, rendering *every* Jew who sympathizes with this country guilty? There is little point in trying to discuss these issues. Israel's expansion resulted from the belligerent Arab fanaticism, which, from 1948 onward, had nothing more to offer the Jews than the promise to "push them into the sea." The Jewish colonialism was one not of conquest but derived etymologically and politically from the Latin term *colonus,* farmer. Israel's "inflexibility" is that of someone who stands with his back to the wall. He is inflexible not for lack of trying but because he has been systematically robbed of the option of being flexible.

---

99 This is a reference to the second verse of the "Harpist's Song" in book 2, chapter 13 of Goethe's *Wilhelm Meister's Apprenticeship* (1795). In the translation of William Edmonstoune Aytoun and Theodore Martin, the relevant passage reads, "Ye leave/The wretch to fall; then yield him up, in woe."

Not that I am unaware of Israel's policy mistakes. But I am much more profoundly and acutely aware of the fact that these mistakes pale into ludicrous insignificance when compared to the realpolitikal indifference of others, of the Russians and the British, the French and the Germans, and likely of tomorrow's Americans too, not to mention the Arabs whose evident compulsion to celebrate their nation-building process by sacrificing the Jew as a burnt offering beggars belief. The altars reek with human gore.[100]

All this is well established, especially where the Jews are concerned. Sacrificing the Jew has considerable pedigree; it is a hallowed tradition. Habits are not easily broken. What, then, might the Week of Brotherliness, which has brought us together, achieve? I have to admit to not being particularly optimistic in this regard. However, I am not just a pessimist by nature but also a believer in the enlightenment by temperament, and my home has always been pretty far to the left on the political map. Hence, I will not let myself be deterred from addressing a few words to my friends on the left. I stand little chance of getting through to those on the right anyway. Even when they present themselves as genuinely pro-Israel, I remain skeptical. I want to stress that I do not doubt that there are some sincere conservatives, maybe even former Nazis, who are earnest about their friendship with the Jews and the state of Israel and whose motivation does not spring exclusively from the desire to exculpate themselves but from the fact that they really have changed their minds on the matter. But as the representative of the social class it serves, the tradition it upholds, and the political legacy it passes on, the right is in no position to develop the sort of unprejudiced attitude toward the Jew one should be able to expect today. It would be absurd to give the circles that funded Hitler only a few decades ago the benefit of the doubt. For them, the fate of the Jews is merely a convenient argument against anything and everything that sets out to challenge our society in its current form. Let us not forget that the calm to which the right aspires is the silence of the grave and its preferred means of maintaining order, oppression.

The Jews, however, including the Israeli Jews, and in fact they in particular, are an element of *fertile disorder*. Wherever ossified structures have been broken down, there they were: from the Young Germany movement to the work of

---

100 This is a line from Goethe's poem "Bride of Corinth" (first published in Schiller's *Musen-Almanach* in 1798), in which Goethe pitted pagan sensualism against Christian chastity. As the female protagonist explains (in the Aytoun and Martin translation), following the conversion of her family to Christianity, "On the cross a Saviour they adore/Victims slay they here/ Neither lamb nor steer/But the altars reek with human gore." The German edition of Arthur Koestler's *Spanish Testament* (1937) bore this line as its title (*Menschenopfer unerhört*).

101 *Junges Deutschland* is an umbrella term for a loose grouping of liberal-minded, politically committed literary figures active in the territories of the German Confederation in the period between the late 1820s and the revolutionary uprisings beginning in March 1848 (the so-called *Vormärz*, i.e., pre-March). In 1835, the authorities banned the writings of most of the authors they identified with the movement.

the Frankfurt School in Germany;[101] as proponents of the Popular Front, then as Sartreans and as structuralists in France; at the heart of the liberal movement in the United States. And as far as the Middle East is concerned, there can be no doubt that it was the Jewish settlers in Palestine and their attempt to create a democratic and socialist society that roused the Arab nation from its deep, centuries-long feudal sleep. Given that it may be misguided but is essentially munificent, the left might want to take this into consideration. It does not bear contemplating that it should be the descendants of the likes of Heine[102] and Börne,[103] of Marx and Rosa Luxemburg, of Erich Mühsam[104] and Gustav Landauer[105] who bear the responsibility for the proliferation of this supposedly virtuous antisemitism, which is the *inevitable outgrowth of the rabid anti-Zionism* that poses a lethal threat for every Jew, no matter where he lives and regardless of his political orientation. This is not hyperbole. Only a shred of imagination is required to envisage what would occur if Israel were destroyed. Fleeing the sword of the prophet Mohammed, the Jewish survivors, retransformed into the mythical wandering Jews, would spread out across the globe, and the world would again react as it did after 1933, when underpopulated states like Canada and Australia closed their doors to the Jews as though they were carriers of the plague. The Jews would again be compelled to take on questionable illegal jobs and engage in obscure financial transactions to make a living. Not even as guest workers would one accept them, especially in times of crisis. The public would be consumed by a time-honored version of the "Jewish Question," which, if we believe Sartre, has never been a Jewish question and was in fact always the antisemites' question. No UN refugee committee would be able to gain ordinary citizenship rights for them anywhere. Anti-Zionism would be dead, to be sure. But crude antisemitism, retrieved from the deepest

---

102 Born to wealthy Jewish parents in Düsseldorf, Heinrich Heine (1797–1856), who converted to Protestantism for pragmatic reasons in 1825 and moved to Paris in 1831, was one of the greatest German-language poets of the nineteenth century. He soon outgrew his romanticist peers to parody and satirize their excessive sentimentality and engage in a razor-sharp critique of the political and social conditions and developments in the German-speaking lands.

103 Like Heine, Ludwig Börne (1786–1837), who came from a Jewish family in Frankfurt (Main), converted to Protestantism for pragmatic reasons and turned his back on Germany to move to Paris (in 1830). He was a prominent journalist and critic and closely associated with the Young Germany movement. Heine and Börne were embroiled in a long-standing, truly vicious fratricidal fracas.

104 Born to Jewish parents in Berlin, Erich Mühsam (1878–1934) was a poet, writer, and anarchist activist imprisoned in 1919 for his role in Munich's short-lived Soviet Republic. Arrested after the *Reichstag* fire at the end of February 1933, he was interned, abused, and tortured in a succession of prisons and camps before being murdered in the Oranienburg concentration camp in July 1934.

105 Born to Jewish parents in Karlsruhe, Gustav Landauer (1870–1919) was a well-known anarchist and pacifist closely associated with Martin Buber and Erich Mühsam. Following the military defeat of the Munich Soviet Republic, he was arrested by Freikorps troops and murdered on his arrival at Stadelheim prison.

depths of the collective unconscious and brought up-to-date, would yet again be retransformed from a contingent historical constellation into a myth, the myth of Ahasver and Shylock.

This would have two principal consequences, and it is high time that we confront them even now. It would wreak total destruction on a group of human beings and amount to the self-destruction of what was up until then the left. The latter is already underway. Even now, we are witnessing how self-avowed "leftist" political groups remain silent when a reprehensible Ugandan despot and paranoiac commits heinous murder[106]; how they fail to protest when the absolute ruler of Libya issues laws stipulating that adulterous women should be stoned[107]; how they have nothing to say about the fact that not one of the grand *chefs historiques* of the Algerian revolution is anywhere to be seen. Ben Bella? He has merely moved from the prisons of the fascist French officers to those of the "socialist" Boumedienne.[108] The left keeps *shtum*. And when it does have something to say, its vocabulary is quite literally de-ranged. It stubbornly insists that the vicious regimes in Libya and Iraq, where communists too are occasionally thrown in jail, are "progressive." Yet in the leftist mythology, Israel, which is not an ideal state, to be sure, but still a commonwealth in which oppositional activities, even anti-national forms of opposition, are permitted, is a "reactionary" country. The problem goes far beyond those eerie dialectics with which everyone and everything can be justified. It is the political witch's 101. It amounts to total conceptual confusion and the ultimate loss of moral and political standards. I am genuinely convinced that the left needs to reinvent itself by revisiting the problem of Israel, i.e., the Jewish problem. Does it still stand for humanistic values? Yes or no? Is its concept of democracy still concerned with universal suffrage and the freedom of speech and assembly, with the *droits de l'homme*,[109] which have, after all, been with us since the French Revolution? Does it still consider *nationalism*, as it always did, a political error born of pigheadedness? Or does it now consider it agreeable wherever it is directed by tyrants against Jews but unjust as soon as Jews, in the face of unbearable pressure, fall into its trap?

Not least: is the left prepared to acknowledge that so-called formal democracy, even though it cannot fully come into its own unless it is complemented by economic democracy, must nevertheless be its priority since without it economic democracy cannot be established? Is, to raise the final question, *justice* still a binding concept for the left? It has been its *raison d'être* since its inception. If the left sacrifices it in order to subscribe to the fetish of revolution, it obliterates itself.

---

106 Idi Amin (1925–2003).
107 Muammar Gaddafi (1942–2011).
108 Following the military coup he led against Algeria's first president, Ahmed Ben Bella (1916–2012), Houari Boumedienne (1932–1978) was the chairman of the Revolutionary Council of Algeria from 1965 to 1976 and the country's second president from 1976 until his death.
109 Translation: human rights.

Which brings us right back to the issue of Israel and the Jews. As Gromyko expressly acknowledged at the time on behalf of the Soviet Union, the establishment of Israel was an act of justice. No one can deny, of course, that this act of restitution entailed injustices for the Arabs, nor is it my intention to conceal this. Even so: the injustice inflicted on the Arabs can be remedied without causing a conflict of global significance. Even now they are not strictly speaking homeless and own two states: Jordan, where they form the majority of the population, and Lebanon, which, jointly with Syria, they control. To be sure, that Israel and the world's Jews should help the Arabs regain their full rights is a legitimate demand. However, the destruction of the Jewish state, and this is what Arab politics in their entirety, from the right to the far left, from the Saudi king to George Habash, aspire to, avowedly or not, would amount to an *irrevocable injustice*. Assuming we are prepared to approach the issue in a matter-of-fact way, it takes no more than a cursory glance at history to recognize this. It is precisely at this point that the left, should it want to find itself again, would need to begin the major task of freeing itself from a number of myths and the vocabulary in whose clutches it finds itself. If it withdrew its unconditional support from the Arabs and gave up on its mechanical yea-saying, it could actually make a contribution to the solution of the Israeli question and the Jewish problem alike. That the overwhelming majority of Israeli Jews, given the unbearable strain they are under, want a reconciliation is not in doubt, nor that the Jews outside Israel understand their position. The strong and wealthy Arab nation has little to fear. In a peaceful Middle East, the dreams of a Greater Israel would disappear of their own accord, as would the permanent fear that plagues diaspora Jewry along with the aggressive response it engenders. The Jews should be free to choose between both options: to assimilate, in keeping with the spirit of the enlightenment, in their host countries or to move to Israel, which still has space enough, even within the borders of 1967, to accommodate what would likely be a limited number of immigrants anyway. This is what the left should be demanding.

The crucial point, to my mind, is that the left, which may well help shape the future spirit and face of the Western world, should abandon its systematic anti-Zionism. For Jews and, therefore, in a historically objective sense, anti-Zionism inevitably bears the repugnant traits of traditional antisemitism. It is almost embarrassing how little insight is required to comprehend this. The young socialists, communists, Maoists, and Trotskyites need only imagine what it would be like if the powers that be told them, "Our issue is not with you but only with World Bolshevism. We do not object to your leftist orientation. However, you may not teach, may not enter the civil service, may not hold public assemblies, and should you form parties, you would be breaking the law." It should be easy enough for them to imagine this situation and recognize that their anti-Zionist affect mobilizes an aggressively Zionist response, on the one hand, and the sort of antisemitic emotions, on the other, that have been part and parcel of the history of the occident and the orient for two millennia and are as much a latent option today as they ever were. Who, if not the left, should be showing any attempt to present this antisemitism perfunctorily masquerading as anti-Zionism as a virtue the ice-cold shoulder?

In contrast to the traditional right with its focus on maintaining the status quo, the left is not entitled to the aforementioned inertia of the heart. It is not entitled to self-mystification, to warped revolutionary mythology, to the abstruse German idealism Thomas Mann once characterized with the words, "If it did not sound like a detestable condonation, it might be said that they [the Nazis] committed their crimes for dreamy idealism."[110] The *left*, if it understands its role correctly, *is a child of the enlightenment*, of the Encyclopédistes, of the great French Revolution, of the intellectual and poetic impact of Lessing, Heine, Börne, Moses Mendelssohn, and Feuerbach. Today more than ever, it should emphatically subscribe to the sentiment Sartre expressed in an interview during the Yom Kippur War: All I know is that in this conflict, three million people are pitted against one hundred million. They should also heed another utterance by Sartre, whose heart, fortunately, still beats on the left, albeit in a ruined body: "Not one Frenchman will be secure so long as a single Jew—in France or *in the world at large*—can fear for his life."[111] Sartre wrote these lines in the immediate aftermath of the Second World War, at a time when the burnt smell of Auschwitz was still in the air and no one in his right mind would have dared to violate the Jews' rights, whether in Palestine, in France, or elsewhere in the world. At the time, no Jew needed to fear for his life simply because he was a Jew. The burnt smell has dissipated over time. In Israel, every Jew, no matter how brave, must fear for his life. And so must every Jew the world over. Maybe only those who have witnessed the homicidal rage of the Third Reich can genuinely appreciate or understand this.

Ladies and gentlemen, the man who stands before you *did* witness that homicidal rage. He was patted down not, as in the fairy tale of Hansel and Gretel, to see whether he had been fattened sufficiently but to ascertain whether he was scrawny enough to be slaughtered. I am appealing to your, to the world's, empathy, above all, however, to your intelligence when I call out: antisemitism, even when it calls itself anti-Zionism, is not virtuous. Far from it. It is an ineradicable "stain on the honor" of civilized humanity.

Please do not take my remarks personally. I know that, regardless of your political orientation, those of you who have come here for the opening of the "week of brotherliness" have done so in genuine good faith. Why else would you have come? However, given that my words may well reach beyond those of us

110 Thomas Mann, *Germany and the Germans* (Washington, DC: Library of Congress, 1945), 14.
111 Jean-Paul Sartre, *Anti-Semite and Jew* (New York: Schocken, 1948), 153.

assembled here and our agreement, in principle, I have opted for the formulations you have heard. The problem of the age-old antisemitism, which presents itself as virtuous and fashionable, goes far beyond anything Christian-Jewish relations could possibly remedy. It concerns the world at large and its history. Wherever and whenever those of us who are in agreement have the slightest opportunity to intervene with our words in the historical trial, which is once again being conducted against the Jews, we are duty bound to make our voices heard: morally, politically, polemically, and with the emotional force that befits a good cause.

Now That I Have Been to Israel

I have since visited Israel for the first time, and I take back nothing. I saw a country in arms, a country as vibrant as it is poor. The class distinctions are disconcerting. In Tel Aviv of all places, I set foot in a Hollywood mansion for the first time. I saw Arabs in the occupied territories and Bedouins who are as proud as the legends lead one to expect. They are poor but own transistor radios that give them access to the voices of the Palestinian Liberation Organization. I spoke to hot-headed anti-Zionist Jews who question the very principles on which the state of Israel rests. This does not, however, prevent them from taking up positions as Israeli university teachers. I spoke to a leftist kibbutznik who has been there for forty years and has long since been transformed from an intellectual into a farmer: a Jewish Israeli farmer who speaks the most pristine German I have heard in a very long time. He told me a melancholy joke about God, who asks the archangel Gabriel about his people in Israel. "They are in good spirits," the sword-bearing angel replied. "Oy vey," the Lord responded, resting his troubled head in his hand, "I fear they are relying on me yet again." The farmer then added in a serious tone, "Maybe it will all end in tears. But the world will have to pay a much higher price for our hides than it realizes." What he meant became clear to me when I subsequently read in the press about Israel's nuclear weapons . . .

A people of conquerors? To be sure, there is a minority who wants to expand the realm and create a Greater Israel. The overwhelming majority certainly does not. Agitated interlocutors spoke to me of the government's "inflexibility" and stressed the need for a far-reaching unilateral gesture. "What is the point of reaching out," others wonder, "if our neighbors are intent on spitting into our hand, at best, and want to chop it off, at worst?" My attention was drawn to the Lebanese example, where Arabs are fighting against Arabs with a brutality we thought was no longer possible. By coincidence I bumped into an "Aryan" German woman who had converted to Judaism and was absolutely convinced that one could not

---

112 This refers to the burial place of the biblical matriarch Rachel, which is located just outside Bethlehem. From 1948 to 1967, it was under Jordanian control and administered by the Islamic waqf.

possibly relinquish Rachel's tomb.[112] And equally by coincidence, I met some gorgeous Arab boys who say shalom when they beg in Bethlehem but in whom one can already discern the determination of the future Palestinian nationalist for whom shalom, peace with the Jews, is inconceivable.

I also saw the occupation. It was not a pretty picture. Armed occupiers inevitably take on the air of a master race. Yet whenever I gave these young Israeli warriors a ride in my car, I saw only utterly exhausted wretches buckling under the weight of their machine guns. Incidentally, and this may be pure coincidence, or the coincidence may reflect a statistical truth, nearly all of them were "black" Jews: their parents had come from Tunisia, Morocco, Yemen, Iraq, and Iran. One of them, whose features were entirely negroid, even came from Libya. By way of an explanation, he simply said, "Gaddafi . . ."

And I saw the fanatics in caftans at the Wailing Wall whom I found extremely ominous, given what I know of their subterranean influence, which weighs heavily enough to prevent the government from agreeing to an internationalization of all these sites of hopeless superstition. Mr. Kissinger, the tragic Jew from Fürth, lurks somewhere in the background, tasked with the implementation of American power politics in the region. The contradictions of the situation are literally maddening. And yet, many think it is entirely straightforward. I spoke to a very young soldier of North African descent who told me that he was paid 150 Israeli pounds (roughly 60 DM) a month and that his family was poor. When I commiserated, he interrupted me and said, "I don't like to fight. But I want to live, so I shall fight." Everything seems to be heading for this fight, for a final reckoning. I can see no solution. The Arabs demand their rights and the Jews theirs. Their claims rule each other out. Bertrand Russell once said, "It was a mistake to settle the Jews in Palestine; but now that this state exists, it would be an even greater mistake to want to get rid of it." One has to be a fool not to see that the Arabs, from the Saudi despot to Arafat and his realpolitik, from Gaddafi to the communist nationalist (or should I say national socialist?) mayor of Nazareth, clearly want to destroy Israel. It is equally clear that the world powers would breathe a sigh of relief if Israel really were made to go away. That the whole constellation could render acute again in a tragic way the "Jewish Question," which has been kept under the lid since Auschwitz, is the ultimate consequence we need to confront even now.

No, I take back nothing. Far from it. Seeing for myself has convinced me of the legitimacy of my position. It has merely robbed me of my last remaining illusions that I might stand the slightest chance of convincing the public of my stance.

9 The Limits of Solidarity: On Diaspora Jewry's Relationship to Israel (1977)

IF THE DIRE portents are anything to go by, it would seem that the political and military forces in the Middle East are preparing for another leap likely to imperil the world. A further war between the tiny state of Israel and the powerful Arab world may end as the previous ones have. Should the Israelis be victorious, it would merely be the prelude to further, ever new armed conflicts. Should the Israeli Jews be defeated, it would inevitably precipitate the physical annihilation of an incalculable number of the country's Jewish inhabitants. One way or the other, because one day the immense economic, military, and potential technological advantage of the Arabs, which is currently still latent to some degree but will become evident in the near or not too distant future, will manifest as its comprehensive historical supremacy, the tragic result would be a catastrophe on a par with Auschwitz. At that point, the God of the Jews will no more be able to protect his people than he was between 1941 and 1945. He is either the Lord and slayer or a weakling or maybe, in his mysteriousness, he is both.

Taking this into account, is this the right point in time to chart on an imaginary moral map the limits of the solidarity that binds diaspora Jewry to Israel? Is it permissible to do so, when an incredibly vicious anti-Zionist/antisemitic campaign based on the tried and tested phantasm of a worldwide conspiracy, perpetrated by the supposedly chosen people against humanity in its entirety, is being acted out in the USSR; when a substantial section of the independent left is intellectually aligning itself with the Streichers and Stürmers of the ostensibly socialist countries to stab the unglamorous and isolated state of Israel in the back (an expression that in this instance would not be cheap hyperbole)?

It certainly is. Unless one is willing to compromise one's commitment to the unity of morality and enlightenment, it is not only permissible but necessary. The fact that Prime Minister Begin, with the Torah in his arm and taking recourse to biblical promises, refers, against all reason and historical insight, to the occupied parts of the Jordanian West Bank as "liberated" and is intent on acting accordingly, this alone would be reason enough for the Jews in the diaspora to review their relationship to Israel. Needless to say, it is inconceivable that they would revoke their pact of solidarity with the country. "Jews and persons classified as Jews according to the Reichs Citizenship Law for the Protection of German Blood" continue to be defined by the non-Jews' gaze. Even where German blood is not at stake, their lot is inextricably linked. Israel is innately their cause, regardless of how they seek shelter—as statesmen, be they American, French, or Austrian; as flustered "leftist" writers desperately clinging to the young; or as pseudo-objective observers of political processes they assume they can contemplate and elucidate *sub specie aeternitatis*.[113] In Harlem, New York, Paris, Buenos Aires, and who knows where else, as soon as push comes to shove, the non-Jews will inform them that they are indeed Jews, half-Jews, quarter-Jews, or in some way "of Jewish kin." The gallows and the bunker notwithstanding, Streicher and his master are still in charge.[114] *As long as a single antisemite exists, all Jews are connected to one another.* The existential pact of solidarity between diaspora Jewry and Israel contains no expiry clause. Even so, or rather, precisely for this reason, the contract partners in the diaspora are duty bound to warn their partner in Israel, obviously in full awareness of the interminable nature of the basic pact between them, but also in the clearest possible terms, of the point at which, and the reasons why, they would be forced not to break (this is inconceivable) but to loosen the bond between them because there are higher, albeit more abstract, commitments at stake.

I have seen (admittedly ambiguous and sketchy) reports on the alleged systematic use of torture against Arab prisoners in Israeli jails and heard the Israelis' sonorous but not entirely convincing denials. I know virtually nothing about what goes on in Israeli prisons. How indeed could I or anyone else have authentic knowledge of these things? Whatever the truth value of the official Israeli or the unverifiable Arab version of events may be, I want to affirm as emphatically as I can, though this in no way draws my existential connection to Israel into question, that I share the anguish of every victim of torture, even if he is an Arab terrorist with blood on his hands. In my value system, for all that I have experienced the full horror of its concretization, the abstract category "human being" outranks the concept "Jew." I urgently call on all Jews who want to be human beings to join me in the radical condemnation of systematic torture. Where barbarism begins, even existential commitments must end. The abstract commandments of *morality* take precedence, they should and must take precedence, over all existential considerations.

Moreover, no moderately rational person can accept that a social commonwealth is based on rabbinic laws, that legends are turned into "history" on which, in turn, current political claims are based. I state this with a lesser degree of moral certitude and do not presume to demand that every Jew should join me in this judgment. I am, however, in agreement with a not insignificant number of intellectually emancipated Jews whose approach is unselfconsciously secular when I say that the "splendor" of Judaism has always been not its (as Freud would say)

---

113 Translation: from a universal perspective.
114 "His master" refers to Hitler.

compulsive neurotic orthodoxy but its ability to transcend traditional modes of being and that its "affliction" (albeit also its mysterious paradoxical mode of survival) has been its grim and rigid adherence to religious tradition. From Heine, Marx, Freud, and Bergson all the way to the young French philosophers and Jewish novelists in New York and Chicago who are more or less our contemporaries, they have all gained prestige and made an impact, not as Jews but as self-transcending Jewish *human beings*.

Consequently, the existence of the state of Israel cannot be justified with recourse to a trove of legends, however dignified its patina, however significant it may be, but only with the human mission embodied by the Jews of the emancipation era and the equally human demand that the Jews, as a free people, should stand on their own free ground given that, to this day, the hospitality of all the various "host peoples" continues to be precarious at best. Human mission? Maybe this is just another unjustified and presumptuous claim? Why should it be the Jews of all the peoples on earth who have had the obligation and noble task bestowed on them to engage in this Promethean task? Does a Jew who speaks of the moral mission of the Jews not succumb to the conceit of election that plays such a prominent role in both overt and covert antisemitic agitation? Well, if one assumes history to be more than the value-free compilation and registration of data concerning events with no inherent meaning, there is no getting around the fact that the survival of the Jews runs counter to history. Where temporality and historicity are presupposed, the Jews are tasked with self-legitimation, in Israel and the diaspora alike. That said, diaspora Jewry, the infamous "world Jewry," if you like, is better equipped to fulfil the task that rests on the Jews' shoulders because it need not resist the temptation of engaging in realpolitik.

All this may sound like unsolicited advice emanating from a safe port: you lot in Tel Aviv and Jerusalem, treat the terrorists who oppose you and who have long since transgressed the bounds of morality with a measure of humanity that goes to the limits of your moral strength and the politically viable. Acknowledge that your freedom can be achieved only *with* your Palestinian cousin, not against him, even though, as yet, he shows no interest in freedom and, in his thirst for revenge, only wants to cut your throat. Even so: accept this advice, for the port from which it comes is anything but safe, and those from whom it comes are standing with their backs to the wall just as much as you are. Do not let the irrevocable solidarity that binds us together become the basis for a communion of two doomed parties in the face of catastrophe. Given the burgeoning antisemitism once again rearing its head the world over, from the extreme right to the radical left, there can be no doubt that the Jews in the diaspora and those in the state of Israel depend on each other. The former cannot hold their heads high unless the latter exists, and the latter cannot manage without the moral support of the former, which will have to be of greater significance in the long run than their material assistance. The donations of the US Hasidim and the lobbying of the Jewish Americans who are afflicted, not only spiritually, by the problem of dual loyalties cannot replace the unconditional support of the enlightened and emancipated Jews in the diaspora who will remain bound to the state of Israel regardless of the circumstances but who can only defend it against a hostile world with a clear conscience as long as it serves as an outpost not of "imperialism," as equally thoughtless and unscrupulous people claim, but of democracy and humanity, both of which are indivisible and neither of which can be compromised.

As yet, the Israeli prime minister and his visitation by biblical visions notwithstanding, Israel is such an outpost. Compared to most of the states in the Third and Fourth World, the country is a paradise, and this would hold true even if the compromising reports were verified. But for how long? This is the pressing question that concerns not only Israel and the Jews. The answer must come not so much from those who hold positions of responsibility but primarily from those possessed of an actual sense of responsibility.

10 My Jewishness (1978)

AMONG MY INERADICABLE recollections are those of the Christian festivals, notably of midnight mass at Christmas. In fact, with a little effort, I can still recite the Catholic credo by heart. How, then, can I legitimately speak of "my Jewishness"? It simply never existed. By the time I found out, in Vienna, the city of my birth, having been pushed and exiled there from the Upper Austrian provinces, as it were, that such a thing as the Yiddish language existed, I was nineteen. Conversely, my mother's sister, who, like her, had been widowed by the war and lived with us, frequently assured me that she would pray on my behalf to her favorite saint, Saint Anthony, who, she insisted, always helped in the face of extreme adversity. What did it take for me to find the courage not only to speak of "my Jewishness" to you here today but to use every opportunity that presents itself to declare that I *am* a Jew?

My father's parents were both Jewish. I never knew my father, who was born in Hohenems (Vorarlberg), because I was born in 1912 and he enlisted with the Austro-Hungarian monarchy's Tyrolean Rifle regiment in 1914. In 1916, he was killed on the battlefield. When I try to gain a sense of his Jewishness, I arrive at no clear result. It would seem that he paid little attention to the religious congregation of which he was officially a member. Indeed, his own father (i.e., my grandfather) had already been quite alienated from the Jewish tradition.

My mother's case was more complicated. She was a Christian, though not, as I later found out, of "purely Aryan" descent. She invoked Jesus, Mary, and Joseph several times a day, which in her native dialect sounded like "Yessusmarrandyawseph." She rarely went to church, only on the high holidays. The prayer she taught me was short: "Dear Lord, make me pious that I might go to heaven." I mumbled this to myself in the evenings until I was about nine. Then I gave up and did not become pious. Hence, the doors of heaven will remain closed to me. Occasionally, my mother would use one Jewish word, the only one I ever heard her say: *nebekh*. Our situation offered plenty of grounds to call out either *Yessusmarrandyawseph* or *nebekh*. We were a proletarianized middle-class family, *nebekh*, and neither Jesus nor Mary or Joseph showed any inclination to take mercy on us. I knew all about my ancestry, but there was never any talk of Jews. Not that anything was hidden from me—matters Jewish just never came up.

After we moved from provincial Upper Austria to Vienna, where antisemitism was a fact of life and the swastika loomed, I began to educate myself. I read whatever I could get my hands on: from Langbehn[115] to Moeller van den Bruck[116] and Hans Blüher, from Houston Stewart Chamberlain[117] to, alas, Gottfried Feder, the vanquisher of the bondage to interest,[118] Rosenberg's *Myth of the Twentieth Century* and even Hitler's *Mein Kampf.* I absorbed all this repulsive stuff in an extremely ambivalent state of mind. On the one hand, it gradually began to dawn on me that these people had undertaken all the requisite intellectual preparatory work to bring about my downfall and that of my kind. Hence, I read their texts with loathing and hostile agitation. On the other hand, I wanted at any price to be "objective," suppressed my burning rage and imposed an intellectual detachment on myself of which I have long known that it was simply a form of psychological repression. It was a perfectly impossible *éducation sentimentale* for a young Jew . . . a Jew?[119] Indeed, because I gradually began to grasp that I myself, as a *Jew,* was the object of my studies, even though, due to chance and my upbringing, I had had little social interaction with "genuine" Jews who were fully aware of their predicament and politically alert. Did I actively avoid their company? I have to admit that I can no longer remember. It has been such a long time since, and I can no longer determine the extent to which my social habits were shaped by semiconscious choice or by fate. It seems to me that, at nineteen, my mental makeup was still shaped entirely by the dullness of provincial life.

In the summer of 1932—Papen was already in power in Germany, and for us in Austria, clerical fascism loomed large—a decisive event transpired in my life that outweighed the impact of all the good and not so good reading material and all my perplexity and provinciality: I fell in love with the girl who would later become my first wife. She had the snow-white and slightly freckled complexion of the genuine redhead; a tiny snub nose; an extremely beautiful, large mouth; and immaculate

---

115 With his best-selling *Rembrandt as Educator* (1890), Julius Langbehn (1851–1907) became one of the best-known German proponents of cultural pessimism and the critique of modern civilization. While the first edition of the book was free of explicit antisemitism, he increasingly infused his cultural pessimism with antisemitism in subsequent editions.

116 Arthur Moeller van den Bruck (1876–1925) was a political writer and precursor of National Socialism best known for his book *The Third Reich* (1923). He rejected Hitler on the grounds that he was too common.

117 As an adult, British-born Houston Stewart Chamberlain (1855–1927) lived first in Vienna and subsequently, following his marriage to Eva von Bülow, née Wagner, in Bayreuth. His two-volume *Foundations of the Nineteenth Century* (published in German in 1899) was one of the best-known works devoted to the propagation of racializing antisemitism.

118 The engineer and economist Gottfried Feder (1883–1941), one of Hitler's early mentors and a long-standing Nazi official, propagated a crass form of innately antisemitic anti-capitalism. His landmark slogan was the call to "break the bondage to interest" ("*Brechung der Zinsknechtschaft*").

119 Reference to the novel *L'Éducation sentimentale* (1869) by Gustave Flaubert (1821–1880). In it, Flaubert portrays (and in part satirizes) the attempts of a young male character to find his way among a number of competing influences and allegiances.

teeth. She was eighteen years old and came from Graz. Her dialect was very similar to my own. She wore a traditional Austrian costume, the so-called Dirndl, which looked wondrously good on her. When it transpired that she was entirely of Jewish descent and religious at that, indeed, that her Styrian ancestry was far from unblemished and her father had come to Styria as a Jew from the east, I was profoundly shocked and disoriented. My mother, who treated any woman with whom I was involved as an obnoxious interloper anyway, called her "a Polish Jew girl." My mother's protest notwithstanding, I did not give up on the maiden with the snow-white complexion. I simply ignored her ancestry. To be sure, I wanted to oppose the Nazis, absolutely, but I wanted to do so of my own volition. I was not yet willing to accept the lot of a Jew. Why? Well, the explanation is simple enough. By reading so many National Socialist texts, I had, as Sartre later pointed out in his unsurpassable *Réflexions sur la question juive*,[120] entirely internalized an image of myself that had in fact been impressed on me by my opponents. I was determined to be an enemy of the Nazis and participated in the brawls that were constantly erupting at the University of Vienna at the time. But I wanted to do so of my own volition, not because of my "blood" or "race." Hence, while already turning my back on Carossa and preferring to read Feuchtwanger,[121] my mimicry, if I can call it that, given that my fatuous nativist wholesomeness was real enough, rose to ever new levels of mastery. My hair was blond, my eyes were blue, and I was very good at using them to signal disapproval. The indisputably Jewish nose I have inherited directly from my grandfather had not yet assumed the welcome and unambiguous severity that would later *set a mark* on me. Truth be told, psychologically, my position back then was utterly untenable. I was, and yet was not or no longer, an Austrian who had been brought up a Catholic. The majority, indeed, the overwhelming majority, not only of the German but also of my own Austrian people had expelled me from their community. I ought to have acknowledged this already at the time, if only I had been willing to face up to the *truth*. Then again, what was the truth? Did it lie hidden in my mother's *Yessusmarrandyawsef*, in my recollections of midnight mass or high mass, in my dialect, in my grandfather's Vorarlbergian family tree or his Jewish nose? When I think it over again now, I feel compelled to revise my own distant past and retroactively affirm the nose even then. I mean this in a very specific sense. I know that the word *race* is frowned on. Yet only a fool would deny that human races exist and are distinguished not only

---

120 *Anti-Semite and Jew* (1946).

121 Hans Carossa (1878–1956) was a well-respected physician and conservative literary author who thought of himself as being apolitical. He was greatly revered by the Nazis and did not leave Germany after they came to power. Born into a wealthy Jewish family in Munich, Lion Feuchtwanger (1884–1958) was an influential playwright and novelist particularly well known for his historical novels. Already abroad when the Nazis came to power in Berlin, he did not return to Germany, living first in France and then on the west coast of the United States.

by their physical features (the dark, light, or reddish color of their skin, etc.) but also by their psychological and intellectual characteristics. To be sure, not only can I not prove this, I am also aware of the fact that modern biologists would hardly agree with me. But does the experience of a long life not ultimately count for more than a few laboratory studies, which may well lead to entirely different hypotheses tomorrow? I am entirely convinced, and no transient anthropologists' claim could shake this conviction, that my intellect and my mental makeup are Jewish, not so much as a result of my upbringing and social environment, both of which could hardly have been less Jewish, but by birth. If anyone now wants to call me a wicked racist, so be it!

Chronologically, I have gotten rather ahead of myself. I absolutely need to mention a date of crucial significance to my life: 1935. The Nuremberg Reichs Citizenship Law, which I read about in a café in Vienna and whose text I soon knew by heart, finally drove home the point that for the Nazis, and not just for the most enraged among them but for the majority of Germans and Austrians, I was a Jew or, rather, as the law stipulated, "classified as a Jew." I did also make one attempt to read Graetz's history of the Jews. It bored me, and I have not given it a second chance. My knowledge of biblical history is derived entirely from (and limited to) Thomas Mann's *Joseph* tetralogy.[122] My understanding of history is that of an average European of the kind who, because his "lack of knowledge," as Robert Musil once rather delectably put it when describing himself, "has very many facets to it," assumes that he is well-informed.[123] My notion of history, in other words, is patchy in the extreme, something I have never attempted to change. This also concerns the history of the chosen people. Only once in my life, in the freezing cold winter of 1940–1941, when I was living in the French internment camp in the Pyrenean village of Gurs, have I attended an orthodox Hanukkah celebration. As the chanting of the worshipers turned into stirring and distressed wailing, I felt as though I had been thrust into an alien and rather uncanny world. Standing next to me was the philosopher Georg Grelling.[124] We looked at each other, speechless and, alas, with a measure of embarrassment. The distinguished gentleman from Berlin cleared his throat and said: it is like being in an ethnological museum. To the extent that, as an atheist, I have studied the phenomenon of religion at all, and I should add that "studied" is already something of an exaggeration, it was Christianity that aroused my interest. This is hardly a stretch. After all, being a Christian is about more than believing in God and his son. Being a critical Christian is about more than the elucidation of theological issues; it is about *participating* in our culture. The church was always on my horizon. The

---

122 See footnote 50.
123 Robert Musil, *Diaries, 1899–1941*, ed. Mark Mirsky, trans. Philip Payne (New York: Basic Books, 1998), 462.
124 Here, Améry actually means the philosopher and mathematician Kurt Grelling (1886–1942).

synagogue was something altogether different. Hence, I cannot really speak of my "Jewishness." I am making the case for another concept, which, I am firmly convinced, is infinitely more significant and which I am inalienably and uncompromisingly competent to speak about: *being a Jew*. With this I can neatly pick up my chronological account again. In 1935, I learnt of and interiorized the Nuremberg Laws forever. I became aware of my *being a Jew*. What that meant to me at the time may have been incrementally intensified and rendered more alarming by subsequent experience, but it has not changed substantively. Society wanted me to be a Jew, and I had to accept this verdict. To withdraw into a form of subjectivity that might have permitted me to say that I did not "feel" like a Jew would have amounted to no more than inconsequential, purely private gameplaying. Only a decade later did I read in Sartre's *Réflexions sur la question juive* that a Jew is somebody whom the others consider a Jew. This was precisely my case.

When the thunderbolt struck on March 11, 1938, and my country jubilantly threw itself at the Führer of the Greater German Reich like a bitch in heat who cannot wait to be mounted, I was prepared.[125] I did, however, still need to take one hurdle: my mother. She had made plans of her own. Her first fiancé, who was of unblemished Aryan extraction, was willing to swear that I was actually his rather than my Jewish father's son. A friend of the family who held an important position at the Genealogical Office would make the necessary arrangements. All I needed to do was quickly resolve one tiny little problem: I would have to separate from the Jew girl who, in the meantime, had become my wife. To this day I wonder whether I might have been more amenable to my mother's suggestion if I had been less passionately attached to this dialect-speaking Jewish woman who would have made a perfect poster girl for the promotion of tourism in the Ostmark.[126] I am tempted to succumb to hubris and say: of course not. I would have left my country even if I had not been forced to do so; I would have emigrated as a matter of principle. Yet how incompatible are hubris and the truth! In the interest of the latter, I have to forgo the former. I simply do not know how things might otherwise have turned out. At the time, I was not familiar with the concept of "authenticity," which has come into such widespread use since the war. Even so, I vaguely sensed that a human being cannot live a total lie encompassing his entire personality. I constituted myself as a Jew. Even so, there were still hurdles I was unable to surmount. For instance, I absolutely refused to have the compulsory forename "Israel" written into my papers. I did not apply for a passport because it would have been stamped with a red "J."

---

125 This is a reference to the *Anschluss*, the incorporation of Austria into the Greater German Reich.

126 Ostmark was Austria's official name after it had been incorporated into Nazi Germany.

127 Jewish Committee.

In Antwerp, the first stop on our flight, the *Joodse Komiteit*[127] took care of us. Having never lived among Jews before, I was now surrounded exclusively by Jews, all of whom were compelled by society to focus on nothing other than their Jewishness. To use the jargon of the time, they now formed a community of fate and a *Volksgemeinschaft*.[128] This community certainly proved itself. The wealthy Jewish community in Antwerp treated us like their own children. That I responded to the community washing around me with profound irritation on more than one occasion was equally mean and stupid of me. I found the Yiddish with which I was constantly addressed excruciatingly embarrassing. I had accepted the fact that I was a Jew in principle. Yet in my daily life I failed. I vaguely sensed that a steep learning curve of an altogether different kind still lay ahead, if I was really going to be who I was: a Jew. The instructors and taskmasters were already on their way.

On May 10, 1940, as Germany embarked on her offensive against her Western neighbors, given that I was a German citizen, I was arrested as an enemy alien. We were taken to the distant south of France. In vain we tried to convince the Belgian and French guards that, having left Nazi Germany, we were no foes of the Allies. We were not Germans but Jews. They did not understand. Jews? What was that supposed to mean? Judaism was a religion. Léon Blum too was a Jew. We had nothing to do with Blum. We were *"des boches."*[129] After six weeks, when the French had been beaten, they abruptly and miraculously saw the light. Under the auspices of Hitler's ceasefire commissions, the *"boches"* (i.e., the real Germans) were released, and the French applauded the victors with repugnant servility. The rest of us, the refugees the Reich did not want back, were transformed at one stroke from enemy aliens into burdensome foreigners and, now in full accordance with the Germans' racist notions, before all else: into Jews. The pejorative *"sale juif"* now replaced the earlier *"sale boche."*[130] Evidently, it struck me, and not just me, the aversion against the Jews had been deposited in a much deeper stratum of the French national character than their shallow *"antibochisme."* It became a little clearer to me every day that the Jewishness imposed on me by society was no German phenomenon. It was not just the Nazis who had made a Jew of me. The world wanted me to be a Jew, and I was prepared to do what Sartre later called *"assumer,"* which we might translate, loosely and inadequately, as "take on." I forced myself to feel a sense of solidarity with *every* Jew. We were already immured in a ghetto much like the one to which the world has confined the tiny state of Israel today.

The instructors were soon exchanged. The brutal but ultimately harmless Gardes Mobiles[131] who had insulted us were replaced by their masters from Ger-

---

128 *Volksgemeinschaft* is a highly charged term defining the national community in ethnic/racial terms as a community of descent (rather than in political terms).
129 A pejorative French term for the Germans.
130 Literal translation: dirty Jew.
131 French auxiliary troops.

many. By this time, I had escaped from the internment camp in Gurs, traversed half of France by foot, and made my way to occupied Belgium to find my beloved wife. I joined the Résistance without the slightest heroic stirring, playing only the most modest of roles. Thinking about it now, this may have been my final unconscious attempt to elude the Jewishness I had long since assumed intellectually. The Jews were hounded, caught, arrested, and deported *because they were Jews* and for no other reason. With hindsight it seems to me that I wanted the enemy to detain me, not as a Jew but as a resistance fighter. This was my final, absurd attempt to run away from the lot of my collective. I risked my life disseminating futile leaflets, vaingloriously deluding myself that I was a "fighter" and not one of those people who allowed themselves to be taken to the slaughter like bleating sheep.

Once I was arrested, reality instantly caught up with me. The lackeys were extremely interested in me as long as they assumed I was a German deserter, a soldier, maybe even an officer. As soon as they realized who I was, they threw me on the dung heap. My file had been labelled "subversion of military morale," and as long as they thought I was a renegade, I was questioned at great length. Once they had figured me out, I was no longer of any concern to them. There was no trial. I was subject to the generalized death sentence called *Auschwitz*. What could I add that I have not already covered in my book *Beyond Guilt and Atonement*?[132] Maybe just this: that it was in Auschwitz that my being Jewish attained its final form, which it has maintained to this day. I had been arrested as a *résistant*,[133] to be sure, but in Auschwitz I bore the yellow star and was a Jew like all those who had never dared make a fuss, never mind circulate seditious leaflets. Only in this circle of hell did the relevant distinctions become entirely clear. Like the tattooed numbers they had branded us with, these distinctions etched themselves into our skin. In this abyss, the "Aryan" prisoners, without exception, were, to an extent measurable only in light years, better off than we, the Jews. They beat us up when the fancy caught them. I would do them an injustice were I not to mention that the Poles in particular excelled in this practice in an unforgettable way. They had all internalized the Führer's values because their tradition had conditioned them to do so. They may have been destined to serve as the master race's slaves, but we had already been given over to death. Eventually, we Jews allowed ourselves to be beaten without putting up any resistance. Only once did I respond in kind, in the misguided assumption I could regain my human dignity by doing so. Then I understood that my gesture was pointless. The Jew was the sacrificial animal. He had to drink the cup—to the supremely bitter end. Drinking it became my way of being Jewish. Jewish*ness*, however, was a dif-

---

132 Available in English as *At the Mind's Limits: Contemplations by a Survivor on Auschwitz and Its Realities* (1980).
133 Member of the Résistance.

ferent matter altogether. I learned to understand Yiddish but made no effort to speak the language. Occasionally, some of the *Ostjuden* would gather and sing Yiddish songs whose texts I could more or less understand.[134] I was deeply moved when on one occasion a few of them sang a Zionist song with the refrain: "*Ich fuhr aheim, ich fuhr aheim.*"[135] By *aheim* they meant the Holy Land. For me, the notion of a home or a homeland would henceforth be meaningless. I was a Jew; I wanted, and was meant, to go on being a Jew. Although I returned to Belgium in 1945, became increasingly interested in French culture, fell in love with Paris, and Jean-Paul Sartre became something of a father figure for me, I no longer believed in assimilation. How could it have been any other way? I had once been not so much "assimilated" but, rather, as fully Austrian as the next man. And yet my Jewish lot had caught up with me. I had come back from the dead but found myself more desperately marooned than ever before. How could I possibly imagine that there might be the slightest possibility of my becoming a Frenchman? The language was not the problem. It was the recollections of my childhood and youth, which, shattered and long since putrid though they are, continue to exist in a negative form. Although they are no longer valid, they continue to constitute my past. It was these recollections that made it impossible for me to invent a new present for myself. The perpetual exile I chose was the only form of authenticity I could attain for myself. The fact of my being a Jew closed off all other solutions.

What I have not acquired, however, is a form of Jewish*ness*, in the sense of a historical tradition and a positive existential foundation for my life. The only connection between me and most Jews the world over is a sense of solidarity with the state of Israel, a commitment that has long since ceased to be a duty of which I need to remind myself. Not that I would want to live there. The country is too hot, too loud, in every respect too alien. Nor do I approve of everything that is done there. I abhor the theocratic tendencies, the religiously inflected nationalism. I have only visited the country once for a short period of time and may never return. Yet even though I do not speak their language and could never adopt their way of life, I am inextricably connected to the people who inhabit this unholy spot and who have been abandoned by the rest of the world. For me, Israel is not an auspicious promise, not a biblically legitimized territorial claim, no Holy Land. It is simply the place where survivors have gathered, a state in which every inhabitant still, and for a long time to come, must fear for his life. My solidarity with Israel is a means of staying loyal to those of my comrades who perished.

Time and again I try to distance myself, yet only ever with limited success. I am an acute critic of Israeli policy. Nor do I hesitate when it comes to alienating goodwill and jeopardizing friendships by stating publicly my strong opposition

---

134 Jews of Eastern European origin. The term especially describes Jewish immigrants to Germany.
135 "I'm going home, I'm going home," Yiddish song by David Meyerowitz (1867–1943).

to the current Israeli government, inspired as it is by irrational forms of chauvinism. I have stated vociferously that the man Begin and everything he stands for is anathema to me. Yet when push abruptly comes to shove, and I sense that the desperately flailing little country is under threat, not my Jewishness, to which I cannot take recourse because it does not exist, but the fact of my *being* a Jew becomes paramount. I take sides. *For* Israel. It is of precious little concern to me whether my leftist friends then call me a renegade. It is easy for them: sticking to principles is child's play. I have chosen the tough option. My loyalty to the lot to which I have surrendered is not a clear-cut concept, and he who conforms to it is forced to throw all dogmatic crutches overboard. He stands on shaky ground. No God and no Marx can help him. And certainly no Hegel.

He, *I* can cleave only to an experience whose quality is ineffable. When Israel, which for me is no Holy Land, is under threat, I see flames all around. And I shout "Fire!" I know that my call will die away unheard. Those who are possessed of Jewish*ness* deny me the right to make myself heard, which is only consistent. The others, those who have never personally and physically experienced the threat, will not listen anyway. I cannot condemn them since I myself do not recall the Turkish massacre of the Armenians on a daily basis. People talk about politics and history, about objective developments. I remain fixated, to the bitter end, on this experience. Were I possessed of Jewishness, I could spryly historicize the subjective experience in objective terms and gain closure. This path is closed off to me. The four walls are moving in; the room is becoming smaller. My (involuntary) form of *being* a Jew without Jewish*ness* (which, given my background and environment, I could acquire only at the price of turning my life into a lie) leads to the melancholia I endure every day. While experts would presumably classify it as "neurotic," it strikes me as being the only mood to which I am entitled.

Epilogue

On the Essays' Reception

Irene Heidelberger-Leonard,
editor of the German-language edition of Améry's collected
works and author of his biography The *Philosopher of Auschwitz*

IN STUTTGART, WHERE Jean Améry's German publisher Klett-Cotta is based, a pathway has been named after Jean Améry (Jean-Améry-Weg). The street sign reads, *Jean Améry (Hans Mayer), 1912–1978, Author and Victim of Nazi Persecution.* When, in 1987, Stuttgart's municipal council decided to name the pathway after him, they wanted to convey that nine years after his death, Améry, who had once been expelled from the German-speaking world, was now firmly established as a point of reference in German public life. The writings collected in this volume are a revelation—and not only for Anglophone readers. Jean Améry is renowned the world over for his writings on the Shoah. Four decades after his death, his crucial role in shaping, indeed, arguably in establishing, the German discourse on Auschwitz is widely acknowledged. But who is familiar with his interventions in West German political debate? Who would have anticipated that these very interventions from the last millennium would be quite so topical today? This may seem all the more surprising given that, at the time, the West German public in general and the West German New Left in particular, in whom Améry saw his natural interlocutor, emphatically ignored them. That they slighted him so ignominiously contributed in no small measure to his sense of political and existential homelessness and, ultimately, to his demise.

While Jean Améry thought of himself as an anachronism when he was still alive, it is now clear that with the critique he formulated he was in fact half a century ahead of his time. The analyses he offered and the questions he raised in his essays not only anticipated the very public historians' dispute about Germany's Nazi past of 1987 known as the *Historikerstreit* and the acrimonious exchange between the author Martin Walser and the then chairman of the Central Council of Jews in Germany, Ignaz Bubis, in 2000. He raised crucial issues that have quite recently come to take center stage given the rapid rise of the far-right party AfD (Alternative for Germany), concerning the singularity of the genocide perpetrated against European Jewry, German identity, and the old-new antisemitism. The topicality of the essays collected in this volume is positively frightening. It is almost as though these essays, written by Améry between 1966 and 1978, were in fact prepared specifically for the current situation. They read like an appeal and a warning addressed to today's crisis-ridden Europe and America alike.

How did Jean Améry, who had vowed, even years after his liberation, never to travel to, or even maintain contacts with, Germany and who therefore, for many years, published his texts only in Switzerland, rapidly emerge as the darling of the West German media? It was the Frankfurt Auschwitz trials of 1963 to 1965 that had prompted him to "weigh in with his word." He wanted to relate *his* Auschwitz. When he met the author Helmut Heißenbüttel in Brussels in February 1964 and the opportunity arose to write and broadcast for the Süddeutsche Rundfunk, a major West German public radio station, he took it, gladly but with a guilty conscience. This collaboration continued until his death, and Helmut Heißenbüttel proved a loyal friend indeed. He not only featured all of Améry's books but also had Améry read them on air. Following the enormous impact of the five essays Améry subsequently published as *At the Mind's Limits* (1966) on the German literary scene, other radio stations, including the Westdeutsche Rundfunk, the Norddeutsche Rundfunk, and the Bayerische Rundfunk, also came knocking, and the quality papers were not far behind. Both Karl Korn, one of the editors of the *Frankfurter Allgemeine Zeitung* (FAZ), and, subsequently, Karl Heinz Bohrer, the paper's feature page editor, courted Améry. Given his sense of commitment to the left-leaning *Frankfurter Rundschau* and its features editor Wolfram Schütte, Améry turned them down. Horst Krüger, the long-standing head of the feature section of the intellectually aspirational West German weekly *Die Zeit*, also asked Améry to write for him. All of them, including not least the high-caliber monthly *Merkur*, for whom he wrote more than eighty essays and reviews, were positively thronging him for contributions.

Améry's essays also drew comment from various fellow writers. Alfred Andersch praised *At the Mind's Limits* "as a reference point from which all thought will henceforth have to proceed," calling it a "fundamental document of our time." Nobel laureate Elias Canetti marveled at this "prophet speaking from the vantage of his own corporeality," and the Austrian philosopher Ernst Fischer admired Améry's "intellectual vitality," his "detachment despite being so profoundly affected, his ability to express the ineffable." Améry had demonstrated "the art of distilling honesty, understatement and the entanglement of experience and insight into first-rate prose." Adorno praised him for describing "the changes in the petrogenesis of experience... in a truly admirable way," and Ingeborg Bachmann immortalized him, even while he was still alive, in her most beautiful novella, *Three Paths to the Lake* (1972).

Andersch's prognosis was entirely accurate, and Jean Améry has indeed been a reference point for further reflection. He inspired W. G. Sebald's *Austerlitz* (2001), and Imre Kertész has described his engagement with Améry in the early 1990s as a "revelation." And his essays on what it means to be a Jew have emerged as a crucial point of reference for nonreligious Jews. They were absolutely essential to Améry, and it is entirely appropriate that they frame this collection, not least because they also form the basis for his stance on antisemitism and Zionism. Améry intentionally introduced the German neologism *Judesein* ("being a Jew"), which he juxtaposed to the term *Jewishness*. His focus was not on religion but on the historical, political, and ethical substance of "being a Jew." His account of the formation and exploration of his own identity provides a template for the treatment of other identities constituted historically and socially by heteronomous imposition. It was exclusively in this sense that Améry acknowledged his "being a Jew."

The aporia created by the tension between specific obligations and the impossibility of meeting them prevails in all Améry's essays. Fundamentally, it springs from the need to live on after the experience of torture, after Auschwitz, and the impossibility of doing so. All the obligations and impossibilities in question thus merge in his notion of "being a Jew" because the heteronomously imposed form of "being a Jew" he described was their ultimate cause. The fact that this form of "being a Jew" has no roots in traditional Jewish culture (let alone religion) constitutes its impossibility. Améry's "being Jewish" hinges exclusively on Hitler's Nuremberg Laws. For Améry, the "catastrophe Jew," the number tattooed onto his arm in Auschwitz was the essential expression of his "being a Jew." For him, the number from Auschwitz was both more concise and more meaningful than the Talmud. To underscore his line of argument, Améry drew on Jean-Paul Sartre's conviction, formulated in *Anti-Semite and Jew* (1947), that "it is not the Jewish character that provokes anti-Semitism but, rather . . . the anti-Semite who created the Jew." Put differently: a Jew is somebody whom others consider a Jew.

However, Améry allows the alienation, which this negatively constructed Jew, this dead man on furlough who suffers from an "insidious sickness," experiences in the world to transition into something positive. Jean Améry acknowledged the judgment history had passed on him as a Jew, "but at the same time decided to overcome it by rebelling." Even when his life was threatened in Auschwitz Monowitz, he defied the fellow prisoner and foreman Juszek. In an act of outright rebellion, he fought back when Juszek beat him. As he explained, I "imprinted my dignity on his jaw with my fist. That I, being physically much weaker, ultimately lost the fight . . . was of no further concern to me. Beaten up and in pain, I was pleased with myself." The lethal implications of "being a Jew" are transcended not by disavowing them but by accepting the moral commitment to join forces with all the dispossessed and oppressed: "Without my sense of belonging to the endangered Jews, I would be a refugee giving up on himself in the face of reality."

In 1966, Améry still presented himself as a non-non-Jew because that was how the world categorized him. In 1978, the year of his death, writing the last of the essays presented in this volume, "My Jewishness," which offers a variation on the themes rehearsed in the first essay, he goes one crucial step further. "What did it take," he asks, "for me to find the courage not only to speak of 'my Jewishness' to you here today but to use every opportunity that presents itself to declare that I *am* a Jew?" The double negative of "On the Impossible Obligation to Be a Jew" had given way in this final essay to an unambiguous, positive identification. Améry came to avow his Jewishness and question the value of assimilation. He ultimately transmuted the heteronomous imposition of this identity into an autonomous choice.

Améry's stance on Israel was closely connected to this self-avowal. It too hinged on a paradoxical impossible obligation. He felt no cultural or religious affinity for the country. For him, it was no Holy Land, "and yet: if there is one state and commonwealth on earth whose existence and independence genuinely concerns me, it is Israel." His support for Israel was not an obligation he had entered into voluntarily; it was "existential in nature." He described Israel as a "virtual asylum," and its existence was crucial to his mental equilibrium. Consequently, he also felt personally threatened by the danger Israel faced during the Six-Day War. "The crucial point is this," he explained in "Virtuous Antisemitism": "the existence of a Jewish state whose inhabitants are not just merchants but also farmers, not just intellectuals but also professional soldiers; who are not . . . 'usurers' . . . but, for the most part, craftsmen and industrial or agricultural proletarians, has taught the Jews the world over to hold their heads high." Israel was not only the country in which the Jew was no longer compelled to have his self-image impressed on him by the enemy; it also continued to be a country for "all the humiliated and libeled Jews the world over."

With this stance Améry, who only ever saw himself as a man of the left, made enemies on all fronts. Those on the right denounced him as a Communist, those on the left as a turncoat. Now that he had outed himself as a man of independent thought, the cultural establishment saw their worst suspicions about him comprehensively confirmed. The media's love affair with him was instantly over. Never had he been quite so isolated or felt so abandoned. In the years between 1969 and 1977, neither the Old nor the New Left could make sense of him. Nothing could illustrate the chasm between Améry and the left more clearly than their respective stances on Israel. Unsettled by the key events in Israel's history—the aforementioned Six-Day War of 1967, the Palestinian murder of Israeli athletes at the Munich Olympics of 1972, the Yom Kippur War of 1973, and the events at Entebbe in 1976—he entered the fray with acrimony.

He spoke of *virtuous* antisemitism, ironically, as though antisemitism could ever be virtuous. He meant the antisemitism of the left, which camouflaged itself as anti-Zionism. The student revolt in France brought down de Gaulle; all over Europe the youth protested against the Vietnam War. In West Germany, the *extra-parliamentary opposition* (APO), which formed an integral component of the student movement at the time, grew, and the killing of Benno Ohnesorg by a policeman as well as the legislation passed for a possible state of emergency helped to set the New Left not only against the United States but against the liberal order in general. In all his writings, Jean Améry directly addressed the German youth, the youth "willing to learn . . . and yearning for utopia; in other words: the *leftist* youth."

Back in 1961, at the end of *Geburt der Gegenwart* (The birth of the current world), Améry had already imagined how the youth would reconstitute itself under his tutelage by grappling with the problem of antisemitism. The contempt the Allies had shown the people of the perpetrators after its capitulation and the hope he placed in the young people who were not themselves to blame led him to believe that "everything has been fundamentally transformed," that the dignity of the Jew had been restored for good. For a short moment, he felt able to indulge this illusion. Yet in the late 1960s and 1970s, ideologically deluded and intoxicated with dialectics, this very left was no longer able to distinguish between an endangered democracy and a consolidated one such as West Germany, which it denounced as fascist and opposed lock, stock, and barrel. Améry felt utterly defenseless against this New Left, which decried the "endangered tiny state of Israel," the only democracy in the Middle East, as an imperialist, colonialist enterprise and condemned Zionism as a universal scourge. Having been victimized by the Nazis both for political reasons and as a Jew, he "cannot remain silent when the wretched old antisemitism rears its head again under the guise of anti-Zionism." He had personally experienced "how the Word was made flesh and the Word made flesh eventually turned into heaps of carcasses. . . . Here one is playing with the fire," he warned, "that dug graves for so many in the breezes." Never had he imagined that he would have to speak out against his "natural friends." Befuddled by an incorrect understanding of Adorno's critical theory, the young enthusiasts had entirely betrayed the legacy of the Enlightenment. To be sure, why should one have expected anything else from the old reactionaries who put Speer's memoirs on the best-seller list? But from the left? Yet he was unable to get the New Left to listen to him, and the young leftists never engaged with his reflections on torture or Auschwitz. They disdainfully dismissed his emphasis on the tormentable body, on "the human being, this bundle of vulnerable flesh . . . this poor skin interested in nothing but protection from the freezing cold and the scorching heat." Their obliviousness to his concerns caused him great distress. As Gerhard Scheit has noted, in the context of radical leftist discourse, Améry's emphasis on the human body was unique.

He was not immediately deterred. In 1969, Améry still thought it worth taking on the self-alienated left marching under the slogan "Strike the Zionist dead, make the Near East red." Hateful anti-Israeli slogans of this kind had the potential to pave the way for tomorrow's genocide. How could he make the leftists understand that Israel had to be seen against the bleak backdrop of the great catastrophe?

To be sure, he was just as convinced of the Arabs' right to establish their own state as the leftists were. That the Israeli-Palestinian conflict pitted legitimate claim against legitimate claim by no means implied, however, "that *the two parties are . . . endangered in equal measure.*" As he noted in 1976, in realpolitikal terms, the Arabs were clearly in a much stronger position, given their Petrodollars and infinitely larger numbers. How, he agonized, might one get the New Left to see in Israel the legitimate refuge it was? If the New Left had forgotten about Gromyko's statement before the UN in 1948 that the existence of the Jewish state was a fact of life, which the Arab states needed to acknowledge, this was hardly Israel's fault, Améry pointed out. The Young Left needed to recognize that its anti-Zionist furor was the offspring of centuries of antisemitism, which had by no means been mastered, and should take to heart Sartre's statement that "not one Frenchman will be secure so long as a single Jew—in France or *in the world at large*—can fear for his life." No matter how virtuous the anti-Zionists thought they were, they were in fact anything but. Following the Yom Kippur War, Améry became increasingly despondent and gave up on the revolutionary left, which felt it had found a comrade-in-arms in the poet Erich Fried.

With one last-ditch initiative, he sought to rally his peers and friends from the Academy of the Arts in West Berlin. Yet here too he failed. In a radio essay, "As Forlorn as I Was in Auschwitz," he lamented that he had been unable to get his colleagues at the academy to express their solidarity. They had merely been annoyed by his request. They too were spellbound by the "awakening of the Third World." The Jews' only cheerleaders at the time were the papers published by Axel Springer, for whom the defense of Israel was merely a pretext for his Cold War grandstanding against the Soviet Union. The only voice that might have offered Améry some comfort was that of the Swiss playwright Friedrich Dürrenmatt, who spoke out in support of Israel in a rarely discussed essay, "Correlations" (1974). In it, Dürrenmatt defended Israel as an "existential phenomenon" whose conception reflected the "audacity of human existence." Yet he considered Islam an equally existential phenomenon. The Jews could not be free unless the Arabs too were free. As magnanimous as Dürrenmatt's analysis of the Israeli-Palestinian conflict might seem, Améry noted, it lacked any current relevance.

Améry closely observed the situation in Israel and did not refrain from harsh criticism of specific political developments in the country when he felt it was required. In August 1977, a year before he killed himself, Améry felt compelled to publish an article in *Die Zeit* in which he outlined his grave reservations: "The Limits of Solidarity. On Diaspora Jewry's Relationship to Israel." "Is this the right point in time to chart on an imaginary moral map the limits of the solidarity that binds diaspora Jewry to Israel," he asked, "when a substantial section of the independent left is intellectually aligning itself with the Streichers and Stürmers of the ostensibly socialist countries to stab the unglamorous and isolated state of Israel in the back (an expression that in this instance would not be cheap hyperbole)?" His response was unambiguous: "It certainly is." His serious concerns are even now, the best part of half a century later, no less pertinent. Améry was outraged by the recourse of the then prime minister Menachem Begin to biblical promises and his brazen contention that the territories occupied since the Six-Day War had been "liberated." Nor, as a secular Jew, did he consider it acceptable "that a social commonwealth is based on rabbinic laws, that legends are turned into 'history' on which, in turn, current political claims are based." Israel's justification lay in its humane mission—though, admittedly, diaspora Jewry was better equipped than Israel itself to meet this obligation since it did not need to resist the temptation of engaging in realpolitik. The Jewish diaspora and Israel depended on each other. The upright gait of the Jews in the diaspora hinged on the existence of Israel. One allegation particularly troubled Améry. Having himself been the victim of torture, he was emphatically opposed to the possible torture of Arab detainees in Israeli prisons. "I urgently call on all Jews who want to be human beings to join me in the radical condemnation of systematic torture. Where barbarism begins, even existential commitments must end."

In West Germany, the applause came from the wrong side. He won plaudits from the bourgeois center, while the socialist left so close to his heart ignored him. One can read about this in his essay collection *Unmeisterliche Wanderjahre* (*Lean Journeyman Years*; 1971), where he took issue, on the one hand, with the muddled, disembodied, and sterile rendering of Adorno's theory to which the student left subscribed uncritically and the abstractions of the French structuralists, on the other, who lost sight of the role of human beings as subjects. Yet Améry was no longer interested in confrontation; he withdrew entirely into himself and his isolation. The soliloquy had replaced the disputation. He buried his dreams, his dream of "educating" the German left in line with his ideas and his dream of establishing himself as a recognized German intellectual in France. In his final years, he dreamed a different dream. He yearned for recognition, not as an essayist and certainly not as a professional former concentration camp inmate but as a German poet and novelist. Yet the general reading public showed no appreciation for his literary exploits. As he saw it, *Lefeu, or the Demolition*, his "life's work," had sunk without a trace. When he concluded that *Charles Bovary* would fare no better, he implemented the suicide plan he had devised meticulously years earlier. Raw existential fear had already reverberated in his *Selbstanzeige im Zweifel* (Self-disclosure in two minds), published in 1977: "I am a man of 65 years . . . more perplexed now than I was as a twenty-year-old youth. . . . All the coordinates are being pulled asunder and with it an ego that has long since learnt to distrust itself."

On October 16, 1978, Jean Améry, who, writing *Ressentiments* back in 1965, had still been full of hope because he believed that others would make it possible for him to leave behind the isolation he lamented, was forced to acknowledge that only he himself could bring about his own liberation. The news of his suicide in Salzburg, when it reached the media, was met with considerable consternation, and it transpired that his own assessment of his role had been at odds with that of the German public. Writing in the FAZ to mark the centenary of Améry's birth, Jürg Altwegg called him a "classic author of the future"—which this magisterial thinker of the twentieth century will continue to be since the future will never catch up with him.

Notes on Sources

The translations follow the text of the German-language edition of Améry's collected works. Varying spellings of proper names have been standardized.

"On the Impossible Obligation to Be a Jew" (1966)
Source of translation:
Jean Améry, "Über Zwang und Unmöglichkeit, Jude zu sein," in *Werke* vol. 2, edited by Gerhard Scheit. Stuttgart: Klett-Cotta, 2002, pp. 149–77.

Original publication:
Jean Améry, "Über Zwang und Unmöglichkeit, Jude zu sein," in *Jenseits von Schuld und Sühne*. Munich: Szczesny, 1966, pp. 131–59.

"Between Vietnam and Israel: The Dilemma of Political Commitment" (1967)
Source of translation:
Jean Améry, "Zwischen Vietnam und Israel: Das Dilemma des politischen Engagements," in *Werke* vol. 8, edited by Gerhard Scheit. Stuttgart: Klett-Cotta, 2007, pp. 223–33.

Original publication:
Jean Améry, "Zwischen Vietnam und Israel: Das Dilemma des politischen Engagements," in *Die Weltwoche*, June 9, 1967.

"Virtuous Antisemitism" (1969)
Source of translation:
Jean Améry, "Der ehrbare Antisemitismus," in *Werke* vol. 7, edited by Stephan Steiner. Stuttgart: Klett-Cotta, 2005, pp. 131–40.

Original publication:
Jean Améry, "Der ehrbare Antisemitismus," in *Die Zeit*, July 25, 1969.

"The New Left's Approach to 'Zionism'" (1969)
Source of translation:
Jean Améry, "Die Linke und der 'Zionismus,'" in *Werke* vol. 7, edited by Stephan Steiner. Stuttgart: Klett-Cotta, 2005, pp. 141–50.

Original publication:
Jean Améry, "Die Linke und der 'Zionismus,'" in *Tribüne* 8, no. 32 (1969), pp. 3419–22.

"Jews, Leftists, Leftist Jews: The Changing Contours of a Political Problem" (1973)
Source of translation:
Jean Améry, "Juden, Linke—linke Juden: Ein politisches Problem ändert seine Konturen," in *Werke* vol. 7, edited by Stephan Steiner. Stuttgart: Klett-Cotta, 2005, pp. 151–58.

Original publication:
Jean Améry, "Juden, Linke—linke Juden: Ein politisches Problem ändert seine Konturen," in *Tribüne* 12, no. 46 (1973), pp. 5229–33.

"The New Antisemitism" (1976)
Source of translation:
Jean Améry, "Der neue Antisemitismus," in *Werke* vol. 7, edited by Stephan Steiner. Stuttgart: Klett-Cotta, 2005, pp. 159–67.

Original publication:
Jean Améry, "Der neue Antisemitismus," in *Tribüne* 15, no. 59 (1976), pp. 7010–14.

"Shylock, Kitsch, and Its Hazards" (1976)
Source of translation:
Jean Améry, "Shylock, der Kitsch und die Gefahr," in *Werke* vol. 7, edited by Stephan Steiner. Stuttgart: Klett-Cotta, 2005, pp. 168–71.

Original publication:
Jean Améry, "Shylock, der Kitsch und die Gefahr," in *Die Zeit*, April 9, 1976.

"Virtuous Antisemitism: Address on the Occasion of Jewish-Christian Brotherhood Week" (1976)
Source of translation:
Jean Améry, "Der ehrbare Antisemitismus: Rede zur Woche der Brüderlichkeit," in *Werke* vol. 7, edited by Stephan Steiner. Stuttgart: Klett-Cotta, 2005, pp. 172–99.

Original publication:
Jean Améry, "Der ehrbare Antisemitismus: Rede zur Woche der Brüderlichkeit," in *Merkur* 30, no. 7 (1976), pp. 532–46.

"The Limits of Solidarity: On Diaspora Jewry's Relationship to Israel" (1977)
Source of translation:
Jean Améry, "Grenzen der Solidarität: Die Diaspora-Juden und Israel," in *Werke* vol. 7, edited by Stephan Steiner. Stuttgart: Klett-Cotta, 2005, pp. 200–206.

Original publication:
Jean Améry, "Grenzen einer Solidarität: Kritik eines Diaspora-Juden an Israel," in *Die Zeit*, September 2, 1977.

"My Jewishness" (1978)
Source of translation:
Jean Améry, "Mein Judentum," in *Werke* vol. 7, edited by Stephan Steiner. Stuttgart: Klett-Cotta, 2005, pp. 31–46.

Original publication:
Jean Améry, "Mein Judentum," in Hans Jürgen Schultz, ed. *Mein Judentum* (essay collection based on SDR radio talks). Stuttgart/Berlin: Kreuz Verlag, 1978, pp. 80–89.

Biographical Time Line

October 31, 1912
Améry is born as Hans Chaim Maier in Vienna, Austria. He is the only child of Paul Maier, (July 21, 1883–August 1, 1917) and Valerie Maier, née Goldschmidt (August 31, 1879–July 1, 1939).

1917
His father is killed in the First World War while fighting in the Austro-Hungarian army. Améry and his mother move from Vienna to Bad Ischl, a small town in the Austrian Salzkammergut region, where Valerie Maier runs a guesthouse and a bar.

1923
Améry attends Gymnasium Gmunden as "Johann Mayer." He would later continue to play around with the spelling of his last name, "Maier" or "Mayer."

1924
Améry's mother's guesthouse goes bankrupt, and they move back to Vienna.

1929
Améry moves to Berlin, where he makes ends meet as a casual laborer.

1930–1938
Améry returns to Vienna and trains as a bookseller. During this time he is sponsored by Leopold Langhammer, director of the Viennese Adult Education Center, "Volkshochschule," Leopoldstadt, where Améry attends lectures on philosophy and literature. Since 1932, Améry himself is an associate at the Volkshochschule. He is significantly influenced by philosophers of the Vienna Circle—namely, Moritz Schlick and Rudolph Carnap.

December 5, 1933
Améry resigns from the Jewish community.

1934
Together with his friend Ernst Mayer, Améry edits the literary journal *Die Brücke* (The Bridge).

1934/1935
Améry writes his first novel, *Die Schiffbrüchigen* (The Castaways). Thomas Mann and Robert Musil review the manuscript.

1935
The Nuremberg Laws come into force in Germany. Améry is highly alert to the increasing discrimination against Jews.

November 15, 1937
Améry reenters the Jewish community.

December 12, 1937
Améry marries Regine Berger-Baumgarten (May 16, 1915–April 24, 1944).

March 1938
Austria becomes part of the German Reich.

December 1938
Améry and his wife flee from antisemitic persecution in Austria to Antwerp, Belgium.

May 1940
Germany annexes the Netherlands and Belgium. Améry is arrested, while his wife is able to go into hiding in Brussels. Améry is deported to Camp de Saint-Cyprien (Pyrénées orientales). He manages to escape from the moving train but is arrested again.

July 1940
Améry is handed over to German authorities and subsequently deported to Gurs, an internment camp in southern France.

July 1941
Améry escapes from Gurs. He makes his way through Paris to Brussels. He is reunited with his wife and joins the resistance against the Germans. He distributes anti-Nazi propaganda among the occupiers.

July 23, 1943
Améry is arrested for distributing leaflets. As a political prisoner, he is brought to Fort Breendonck, where he is brutally tortured. When his captors realize that he is Jewish, he is deported to Auschwitz concentration camp in German-occupied Poland.

January 1944
Améry arrives in Auschwitz. He is imprisoned in Auschwitz Monowitz, one of the three main camps in the Auschwitz concentration camp complex.

January 1945
The Germans evacuate Auschwitz Monowitz because of the advancing Red Army. He is forced to march to Gleiwitz II concentration camp. From there, Améry and other surviving prisoners are deported to Mittelbau Dora concentration camp in Germany.

Early April 1945
Prisoners of Mittelbau Dora are deported north. Améry is sent to Bergen-Belsen concentration camp.

April 15, 1945
British soldiers liberate the surviving prisoners of Bergen-Belsen.

April 29, 1945
Améry returns to Brussels. He learns that his wife has died of heart failure. He makes a living by writing commissions. Améry still writes in German but has no intention of publishing anything in Germany or Austria, the countries of the perpetrators.

Fall 1945
Améry meets Jean-Paul Sartre in Brussels. Sartre becomes the most influential philosopher for Améry's thinking after Auschwitz.

April 2, 1955
Améry marries his second wife, Maria Leitner, née Eschenauer (March 20, 1911–2004). The two live in Brussels.

1955
To illustrate his dissociation from German culture, Améry changes his name from the German Hans Mayer to the French Jean Améry.

February 1964
Améry meets Helmut Heißenbüttel, editor at Süddeutscher Rundfunk, a large West German public radio station. He gives Améry the opportunity to record his autobiographically grounded reflections as a Jewish Nazi-victim.

1964–1966
Five autobiographical essays are broadcast by Süddeutscher Rundfunk in Germany.

1966
His essays are published as *Jenseits von Schuld und Sühne* (available in English as *At the Mind's Limits: Contemplations by a Survivor on Auschwitz and Its Realities*). The book's success gives Améry the financial freedom to quit commissions.

1966–1978
Numerous publications and public readings. From 1966 onward various articles addressing antizionism and left-wing antisemitism. Améry also picks up writing novels, such as *Lefeu oder der Abbruch* (*Lefeu, or the Demolition*), published in 1974. Améry's extensive oeuvre, if reprinted, would cover roughly fifteen thousand pages.

1974
Améry attempts suicide but survives. A scathing review of Améry's *Lefeu oder der Abbruch* is published in the German newspaper *Frankfurter Allgemeine Zeitung*. It causes a long-lasting depression.

October 16/17, 1978
Améry takes his own life in a hotel room in Salzburg, Austria.

Contributors

Jean Améry (1912–1978) was born as Hans Chaim Maier (later spelled Mayer) in Vienna. Throughout his life, Améry was a committed writer. He published several novels as well as numerous essays on literature, philosophy, politics, and contemporary history. In 1938, he fled to Belgium to escape antisemitic persecution in his native Austria. After the German invasion of Belgium, he was arrested and deported to Auschwitz. Following the evacuation of Auschwitz, he was held captive in a number of other camps before he was liberated by the British Army at Bergen-Belsen. He then returned to Brussels. As an expression of his alienation from German culture, he subsequently adopted the name Jean Améry (a French anagram of Mayer). While he never contemplated moving back to Austria or to Germany, he became a perceptive observer and critic of postwar German society. For the first two decades after the war, he earned his keep mostly by taking on various writing assignments. It was not until the 1960s that he found an audience for his own writings. His collection of autobiographical essays, *Jenseits von Schuld und Sühne* (translated as *At the Mind's Limits*), was published to considerable acclaim, allowing him henceforth to make a living as an independent author. He was among the first to publicly criticize the rise of antisemitism and anti-Zionism among leftists of various stripes and especially in Germany.

Marlene Gallner studied Political Science, Philosophy, History, Jewish Studies, and Austrian Studies at the Universities of Vienna and Maryland, College Park. While living in Israel in 2010–2011 and 2013, she worked with Shoah survivors from Central Europe and at the Moshe Kantor Database on Antisemitism and Racism at Tel Aviv University. She has been running educational programs in Germany, Austria, and Israel that focus on the history and impact of Nazism and the Shoah since 2012. She is one of the editors of *sans phrase: Zeitschrift für Ideologiekritik*, the Vienna-based biannual German-language journal dedicated to social and cultural analyses in the tradition of Frankfurt school critical theory, and has lectured and published widely on antisemitism, postwar German society, and post-Shoah philosophy. Her recent English-language publications include "Like a Cloud Contains a Storm: Jean Améry's Critique of Anti-Zionism" (*Fathom*, autumn 2016).

Irene Heidelberger-Leonard, Dr. phil., professor emeritus, Université libre de Bruxelles and Honorary Professorial Fellow Queen Mary College, University of London. She is a member of the German Academy for Language and Literature and wrote books on Jean Améry, Günter Grass, Alfred Andersch, Ruth Klüger, Jurek Becker, Peter Weiss, Thomas Bernhard, Ingeborg Bachmann, and W. G. Sebald. Last published: *Imre Kertész: Leben und Werk* (Göttingen, 2015). She is the author of Améry's biography *The Philosopher of Auschwitz: Jean Améry and Living with the Holocaust*. It was named the Nonfiction Book of the Year by the German Cultural Foundation in 2004, won the Raymond Aron Prize in 2004, and was awarded the Einhard Prize for Outstanding European Biography in 2005. Irene Heidelberger-Leonard is the editor of the nine-volume German-language edition of Jean Améry's collected works.

Alvin H. Rosenfeld is Professor of English and Jewish Studies at Indiana University, Bloomington. He received his PhD from Brown University in 1967 and has taught at Indiana University since 1968. He holds the Irving M. Glazer Chair in Jewish Studies and is director of the university's Institute for the Study of Contemporary Antisemitism. He founded Indiana University's well-regarded Borns Jewish Studies program and served as its director for thirty years. He has been honored with the Indiana University Distinguished Service Award and also the Provost's Medal "in recognition of sustained academic excellence, vision, and leadership resulting in lasting and widespread impact." Professor Rosenfeld has served as an editorial board member of various scholarly journals, including *Holocaust and Genocide Studies* and *Antisemitism Studies*. He has also been a board member and scholarly consultant to various national and international institutions and organizations, including the Anti-Defamation League, the American Jewish Committee, and the Conference on Material Claims against Germany. He held a five-year presidential appointment on the United States Holocaust Memorial Council (2002–2007) and also served on the US Holocaust Memorial Museum's executive committee.

Index